MAGIC

MAGIC
FOR MEN

By Bruno Meyer
with Manny Diez

Straz Publications
6920 Roosevelt Way NE, #279
Seattle, WA 98115

Edited by Luana Ewing
Cover art and design by Tim Oldfield

ISBN 0-9725223-0-1

First paperback printing October 2002

Visit our website at: www.magicformen.com

Published in the United States of America

For the uplifting of the male spirit

Acknowledgments

Without these three incredible women, this book would not have been written: Sharon Regie Maynard, mystic and shaman, with gratitude for her dimensional work and T.A.G. teams.

Laurie Ray, a true star child, thank you for your heart.

Mary Leary, alchemist extraordinaire, thank you for your friendship.

I

Disclaimer: Along the way in this book, the author offers a series of exercises designed to aid the reader in achieving an elevated mental state. While none of these in any way require a high degree of physical exertion, if you have any medical conditions that you feel might be aggravated by performing these exercises, then please consult with your doctor first.

II

Table of Contents

Chapter 1

THE LAW OF ATTRACTION

Intention

I intend and know I deserve

This book is not a history of magic as you commonly understand it. Rather, it is a series of simple exercises and concepts, which if you use them and understand them, will help you to bring inner magic into your daily existence. They will help you to further your wishes, ideas and goals, to bring them to fruition, and to make what had been dreams become reality.

You're going to learn how to wake up the Great Magician that has been too long dormant inside you.

You're going to learn that daydreaming your most outrageous desires, and opening your mind and creating new realities, is not only okay, but healthy and fun!

You'll learn how to tap into the world of your creative imaginings. What it all comes down to, my friend, is: use it or lose it!

You're watching too many sports on TV. Living your life vicariously through other people's games, through someone else's experiences, when you should be fully experiencing your life through your own self-generated excitement!

By placing yourself in this third person spectator role, you are, whether you realize it or not, stultifying your mental life, number one. Number two, it causes obesity when overindulged, and number three, if that's the only form of excitement you're part of, it's not going to do a hell of a lot for your sex life either.

Bottom line on what is probably your favorite pastime: the electronic frequencies generated by television will *flatline* your brain—that same type of line you've seen on medical shows that indicate the patient has just died. Is that what you want for *your* brain?

Your imagination is your freedom. Don't toss it into the fire, onto the mindless pile of sports and games and videos, and someone else's reality, someone else's show. Consider this: how about being your own hero in your own show by learning how to use your own imagination? An exercise that will free you to become whatever you can imagine!

As you learn to live the magic, your life will become more synchronistic, and things will start happening that would not be considered normal by other people.

This mind we're talking about is infinite. To liberate it you're going to have to put aside your very limited mechanical computer, and begin learning to use your own organic computer, which is the highest biological tech unit out there. By doing that, you will take your first steps toward Manifestation.

We live in a world of "obey, consume and die." How about an alternative? How about speaking, manifesting and living? Remember: you do have choices, and this is a choice you have on this planet, right now—which you really need to make, because the current reality is so terribly damaging to your masculine spirit. Manifest your choices! Create your own reality!

Concentrate on what you want, and you will get it. You have the ability to change your reality, but first, obviously, you have to know what that picture of reality is. You have to observe it. Really see it as clearly as you can. Be brutally objective. Observe what you're doing and saying. How you're responding to the incidents life surprises you with. Once you have done this, open your imagination and take your first steps toward the exciting process of manifesting.

We inhabit the Technologically Conscious age, so consider playing a new game: *Intendo*. "I intend." The possibilities are endless, exciting, and yes, fun! "I intend to enjoy life!" "I intend sovereignty!" "I intend to be comfortable with wealth."

The simple act of desiring an intention will become your most powerful tool because it has no limits, and best of all…it's totally yours! There's nobody saying, "Hey! You can't do that!"

You have a unique genetic signature: your DNA code, that famous double helix that is your specific life blueprint. No other living creature has your code, so while the genetic differences between you and your fellow human beings might be infinitesimally small, there is only one you.

You begin changing your reality through intentions. You can do this first thing in the morning by saying, "I intend health and vitality." This is the first step in how you'll start programming your brain—instead of that other computer you spend so much time on. By making forceful, dynamic intentions every day!

You will learn to be more receptive to your "gut instincts," the ones women are so expert at using. You have a heart. Listen to it! We're talking about training your mental, physical and spiritual body. Consider it an evolutionary step forward along this journey we are embarking upon right now, and at the same time it is a visit backward to a time when men had finely tuned bodies and instincts that were in perfect harmony with their spirits. You can do that again!

You Attract What You Transmit

We're talking about the transmutation of your experiences as a male. If you walk into a bar, or any such scene, with your electromagnetic system beaming out, "I'm a loser; I'm a trickster; I'm dishonest, and whoever gets involved with me is going to have a really bad time," who do you think you will attract?

Without changing, and this goes back to your picture of reality we talked about, who are you going to attract? If you don't know what your picture of reality is, you're going to pick up whoever is receiving on your frequency. And the whole thing is frequency. The entire planet is frequency. "Birds of a feather flock together."

If you're a material guy, and you walk into a bar, guess who you're going to attract? A material girl! "Gee, and all the broad wanted was my money!"

This is truly about transmuting your energy field. Do you want to attract something different? Become something different. Change your energy field. Change it into something new and you'll attract someone new.

6

Chapter 2

HOW TO ACCESS FEELINGS

(The Ultimate Turn-on for Women)

Intention

I intend to live with passion

You've heard about "Female Intuition?" Is there a male equivalent? No? You sure? How about paying more attention to your gut instincts? You get them all the time, but you tend to ignore them. You feel them in personal and social relationships, in business related affairs; you feel them, but you ignore them.

Where along the line did you lose your psychic ability? Where along the line did you lose your ability to feel? Far more important, how can you get them back?

How to Access Feelings

To begin with, you must learn to become *more aware*. No matter how faint or fragile the thread of a thought is or feels, observe and take *notice* of it. This is working magic, flexing your intuition. You become *aware* of the idea at the moment of its conception or impulse. Practicing this simple technique will become your true ally.

If you were incredibly lucky, your mother, your sister, or perhaps another male member of your family or a friend, actually helped you extend those Life Lessons. Encouraged you to explore them. If so, you were in the very fortunate minority. So if you ever walked into a place and had an overwhelming feeling of, "Let's get out of here," who could you share that with? Certainly none of the men you knew. And do you ever remember your dad asking, "So, son: what did you dream about last night?" Right.

We have always found it much easier to talk to women on such matters. We can converse with them on a much deeper level because there's no fear of talking about things that are off limits for men to talk about. How come? Because we *men* have a very rough time delving into these subjects among ourselves. Basically, it embarrasses the shit out of us, because to actually bring the subject up at all would make us the object of some rather curious looks, and raise some less than flattering questions about our "manhood."

Sharing such incidents, feelings, is an outside nature to most people, certainly to most men. But not so with women. For them it's quite natural, very much a part of who and what they are.

As you go through this book, you'll find passages, exercises, intentions that will help you regain what was once also a natural part of you--the part of you that feels! Then there's the male affection thing...

In our society, the United States of America, men are pro- grammed to not show affection toward each other, whereas in European and Latin countries, males publicly embrace; even kissing is okay. What's the connection between that and our losing our ability to feel? Easy. It's another inhibiting factor men get saddled with. Another, because there are others as well.

How about men not being free to show their emotions in public? It's a proven fact that men feel emotions just as deeply, and sometimes more deeply, than women; but from when we were little, we were told that, "big boys don't cry." And you wonder why men tend to inhibit feelings? Flashes of intuition?

Did your father hug you? Did the men in your family show open love and caring toward each other? Not if you were reared in the traditional American home. At what tender age did you begin to get cut off from normal displays of affection with your brothers, relatives, male buddies? It happens to all little boys, and the long-term damage can be devastating. Hitting, punching and kicking were okay because that's what *men* did.

Here's what I want you to do. Find a male buddy. Go play a little one-on-one. Three-on-three would be even better. No bas- ketball court handy? Toss a football. Throw a baseball back and forth. Enjoy the lovely arc as the football sails toward your friend. The tight spiral. How good it feels when the baseball hits your mitt, your hands. This is your show! One *you've* created!

By these simple acts you're creating your own energy, your own excitement! Your own magic! Sure as hell beats sitting around watching, doesn't it?

How about déjà vu? You've experienced some of those moments, right? Did you, even once, share those feelings with a guy? Yeah, didn't think so. And why not? Maybe because it's a "female thing." It all comes down to letting what you feel show. You'll get the hang of it as you express yourself more often.

There are some professions where men don't have any problems freely expressing their feminine sides. These are primarily in the artistic fields. Artists have always had access to more than just a single aspect of themselves, and we're talking about male artists. They have no problem expressing their feelings, unleashing their creativity, both of which serve to enhance their performances. This is, by the way, a freedom that carries over into their personal lives as well. A lack of inhibition that allows them to more fully explore and enjoy those moments of emotional exhilaration that most men would do their very best to suppress. There's also a geographical element at work here.

A male reaction in one country might be considered female in another. In certain African tribes the males dress up with lipstick and flamboyant costumes. They preen; they exhibit themselves for the women. They dance for them. The women are plainly dressed, and have no makeup on. They are watching and choosing.

The same holds true in nature. Look at the male animals. The magnificent plumed array of the peacock. The majestic head of the male lion. These male creatures have no problem showing themselves off, because by so doing so, they are making themselves more attractive to the females.

By accepting that you are more than you thought, by allowing yourself the freedom to be that multifaceted person, the freedom to not only become more fully aware of your feelings, your intuition, your emotions—all of them—you will begin the magical process of liberating your true self, your true being.

You're Standing on My Foot!

There will be some revealing surprises. By opening your solar plexus, your feeling center, you'll become more sensitive, more aware of what's going on around you, and especially more sensitive to those things and events that impact on you directly. I'll give you a classic case that is not as isolated as you might think.

On his wedding day, alone, looking at himself in the full length mirror, wearing whatever costume he's selected for the occasion, the groom sees himself and suddenly gets an over-powering feeling that no, he doesn't feel right about going through with this. Almost as if an elephant was standing on his foot, and it hurts. "Excuse me. You're standing on my foot."

In that moment, in that illuminating flash of intuition, that guy knows this is a big mistake. What does he do? He walks out of the room, down the aisle, and gets married. And there's a real good chance he'll regret it. But too late. Oh, and by the way, this happens to brides just as often, and they go ahead and get married as well.

It probably never occurred to this man to simply ask the elephant to remove his foot, because he might not have come to this moment in time when he could make such a simple request.

The bride will, of course, be devastated. Her parents and family and friends will be devastated. Her father may come after him with a heavy metal object. The guests will be stunned. His friends will think he's gone nuts.

It would, of course, be much better if this moment of enlightenment came two or three days before the wedding. Not nearly so messy or embarrassing. But what's important here is hearing the voice, feeling the sensation in your gut that says, this is not going to work out, and then having the courage to step back and call it off. Ask the elephant to move before it's too late.

To avoid finding yourself in such a position--and I'm not just talking about something as dramatic as calling off a wedding--all you have to do is use your intuition before events come to the point of causing emotional pain for you and for others. You can spare yourself, and everyone else, this discomfort by just asking the elephant to please remove his foot.

The main purpose of this book is to help you to increase your sensitivity—in all areas. In your life. At your job. With your family. With the people you come into daily contact with.

Chapter 3

BRING BACK GALLANTRY

Intention

I intend a joyful life

Gal-lant-ry. 1. Nobility of spirit or action; great courage.
2. Chivalrous attention toward women. 3. Bold or colorful
display in appearance or dress.

Did you see the film *Don Juan de Marco* with Johnny Depp?
In it, Depp does more than simply believe he's really Don Juan.
He *becomes* his idol. He lives a life parallel to his real existence.

At one point in the film, he shares his flights of romantic fantasy with his psychiatrist. The marvelous romantic adventures this
gentleman hears from his patient affects the doctor. The result?
The beguiled doctor goes home to his wife and brings the Don
Juan spirit with him. His wife is at first startled, but then has no
problem adjusting to this delightful new man. They both enjoy
being part of the fantasy, having a really good time.

Do you remember how men dressed in those days? All
velvets and silks? Can you imagine a formal affair back then
where all the men turned up wearing pretty much the same
outfit? We call them tuxedos. How times have changed.

We're talking about our clothing here because it's the most
obvious expression of how routine our lives have become.
Society, where we work, where we go, all conspire to dictate
how we should dress. And yes, there are those occasions where
standards relax and we can put on an outfit that speaks of who
we are, how we're feeling, what we want to express. Sadly, those
times are few and far between. We remain, for the most part,
trapped in routines that tend to sap our creative nature. Isn't it
time we explored other options, and not just in dress?

What we want to explore now is: how to *unroutinize* our
lives. Okay. Remember how much fun you had when you were a
kid--playing games, making up fantasy worlds? Who says you
can't do that again, at least once in a while?

We're not suggesting you become Peter Pan, but that you
find opportunities, from time to time, to unleash your adventurous spirit! When a woman sees a man who is unafraid of showing the adventurous child in him, it isn't the child she's attracted
to, but rather to the man who's confident enough, powerful

enough, and relaxed enough to share that youthful spirit and not be afraid of "what others will think." Who remembers what being a child is all about? It takes a man with guts to pull that off. It creates magic, and for women, irresistibility.

Let's face it: having to get up five days a week, get to work, go to work; that tends to suck a great deal of romance out of your life. The same goes for her. How about putting some fun back into it? People, including women, are drawn to a happy person, someone who is fun to be around. Humor is a powerful aphrodisiac, and women are attracted to a man who makes them laugh, to a man who sees the absurdity of life, and has happily decided to do something about it.

Use your creative imagination. You'll be amazed at the results! Do it first for yourself, and even then you'll notice the differences. Little subtle changes that might make you laugh out loud when you're alone. Give yourself the sheer pleasure of inhabiting your version of the Don Juan syndrome and watch what happens. Not only will you notice the differences in you, but so will everyone you come into contact with!

Why not exercise your youthful charm and playful boyhood? Why should kids have all the fun? The great thing about the inner child is that he never gets older! You can be gallant for that one moment when you hold open a door for the woman right behind you coming out of a store. You can be gallant when you let a lady have your seat on a bus or subway. As you go through each day, there are numerous small acts of gallantry you can perform that will give both you and the object of your gallantry a nice warm feeling.

When you go to meet her for the first time, bring a flower, bring a rose, bring a bouquet you picked on your way to her place. It doesn't matter if they're just a haphazard collection of weeds with the occasional tiny blossom among them. It's a small act of gallantry that shows her you cared enough to make this simple gesture in honor of this special occasion.

"I intend fun!" By simply saying that, you invite the spirit of fun into your being. If you begin this first meeting with this new lady with that spirit in your heart, everything will go much easier because there will be less pressure. You don't have to win her heart tonight. You don't have to captivate her soul. No! All you are doing is having fun! And guess what? After less than 60 seconds in your gallant, fun company, she'll sense what's going on and she'll begin to relax too!

I'm not suggesting that you play an unreal role, be somebody you're not. That would be phony, and ultimately uncomfortable. What I am saying is, give yourself the freedom to be another facet of who you are. There are many personalities inside each of us. When we were kids, we had no trouble trotting them out, remember? So what's happened? Where along the line did we become so inhibited? Where along the line did we begin having less fun? When did we stop using our imaginations?

Open your mind; liberate yourself! There is nothing wrong with becoming a free, youthful spirit once in a while. And there is never a time when you should inhibit your sense of gallantry!

Lighten up, guys. Being a "Man" in a man's world can get terminally boring. It's all about guns, and sports, and cars...and work, and getting laid, and bullshit. The good news is, you can liberate yourself from that world any time you like. You can do that by exercising your imagination. You can do that by creating, by actually *creating* a new existence, a new place you can come to any time you like. You make a new picture of reality. No dull routine. Just fun!

You can exercise the ancient art of storytelling as a way of rekindling your imagination in a kind of romantic role-playing way. Remember, a woman falls in love through her ears. We're not suggesting you walk down the street with your girlfriend reading from prose and poetry books. However, it might be a good idea to start reading a few such books to stimulate your use of a new vocabulary you're going to be learning. A romantic one. A gallant one.

Do you want to capture a woman's attention? Be gallant and be all that that quality implies. Make the small gestures. Give her a rose. Just one. Create magic for her. For yourself!

We just talked about how humor can turn a woman on; it lightens up the moment. But there is something else women, any woman, will also find exciting, and this one is easy. Listen to her. I mean, *really* listen. This is not something you can fake. That implies being dishonest, and if she catches you doing that, you've just lost her trust.

If you, with sincerity and charm, listen to a woman, it's an absolute aphrodisiac for her. If you don't think she's got gorgeous eyes, don't say that she does. However, if you will listen to her for even a short period of time, you're going to figure out exactly what her interests are and where she's coming from. Find the aspects of that woman that are attractive to you and turn you on--without being dishonest. Whether you can't stop thinking about her ankle, or her hair or her eyes; it doesn't matter. But to voice that is an incredible aphrodisiac to her. Just to voice the thought. Anyway, use these tools, and I think you will begin to enjoy the process, and the results will be pretty astounding.

You can begin the observation process the first time you go to her house to pick her up. If you walk into her home and are able to determine that she is an extremely independent lady, then you might think twice about overwhelming her with certain kinds of gallantry. This type of woman might not like having doors opened for her, chairs pulled back. There are women today who find such acts as signs of attempted male dominance, so get your internal antenna working and figure out just what kind of woman you're with.

If on this initial visit you notice that she has prints of Egypt, or of wolves on her wall, that's certainly a clue as to what interests her. So look around; observe her habitat. Even the smallest details will give you a quick insight about who this woman is. What kinds of books are on her shelf? Fact? Fiction? Romance? Art? Maybe there's a Bible on her coffee table. This is not rocket science here. Look. Observe. Draw conclusions so that later when you comment on a subject you know does interest her, she's going to think you're a very intuitive person, and that's a good beginning.

For our purposes, for our demonstrations of gallantry, let's get to most women today: they haven't had a man do anything remotely gallant for them in a long time. Such a lady will be charmed by even the smallest acts that let her know she's in the company of a considerate man. And guess what? If she feels that way about you right from the start, she's going to further assume you'll be gracious and considerate in other areas as well.

Remember the Intention for the last chapter?..."I intend to live with passion!" Those are not just six words strung out to fill up space. It's crucial that you get a clear image of exactly what the word "intend" means. It isn't "I hope." Hoping something will happen means nothing. It's weak; it's wishful thinking. "Gee, I hope I get that raise." "Gee, I hope she likes me." NO! By *intending* you leave no room for doubt. "I intend to succeed!" "I intend to have fun!" "I intend a great romance!" A huge difference.

In this case, you've intended to have fun, so do that! Enjoy this exciting new process of how you're going to be leading your life from now on! Enjoy the magic!

Let's Pretend

Social interaction requires your meeting other people. That means meeting other people who can also enjoy the fun of liberating themselves from the usual stultifying routines.

Create an atmosphere, a fun atmosphere. You do that by exercising your imagination, by creating a fantasy, an exciting new reality others will want to be a part of. And you can bring them into your fantasy *if*–and this is a major if—*if* you truly believe this fantasy yourself, which entails some acting.

I know what you're thinking. But isn't acting something phony? No! It's not! Did you ever see a good play? If there were talented actors on that stage, you were soon drawn into the reality they were creating up there. Their emotions were real. Their pain was real. Pain and emotions they made you feel.

Social interaction is, of itself, an act. This doesn't mean that you're going to be a dishonest person. It only means that you are going to open up your life. You are going to open it up to new realities, and the only way you can do that is by exercising the neurons in your brain. You've got to open up new pathways. Does it matter at first whether you're doing it as an acting job? No, it doesn't. All that does matter is that you believe in yourself, in your performance.

You know what those actors we just talked about did before they ever set foot on that stage? They rehearsed a lot. You can't give a great performance without rehearsing; there's nobody out there who can do that. So do it. Rehearse. Do it at home; do it in front of your mirror. Become this marvelous new man you *intend* to become. Will you feel silly doing that? You bet. Will it be fun doing that? You bet. Just think of the possibilities! My God! You are exercising this amazing new freedom of being able to create anyone you'd like to be!

Once you have fashioned this new person, it will no longer be an act. He will be you. It's all a game. The whole thing is a game, so why not enjoy it, every single minute of it! The lighter you are, the less you're going to hurt yourself or anybody else.

Now, if along the way the lady falls for you, well hey; it's happened before and it will happen again. And hopefully this book will inspire a few to fall for you. Not because you're a phony; not because you're out there to do somebody in, but because you want to do something different, and you want to have fun doing it. And why not? See yourself as that swashbuckler; see yourself as whoever it is that turns you on. Bring back some magic and some gallantry and...some intrigue!! Fascinating thing, intrigue.

So what the hell is intrigue anyway? It's the unexpected. It's a surprise. It's mysterious. But most of all, it's fun! It's to say something she's never heard before. "If you were the Creator, would you have put all those stars, all those planets, all those universes up there, or would you have left it blank?"

As you get further into this book, you'll be asked to intend many things. Not *hope* you can do something, but *intend* it. To do that thing, that exercise, that intention with passion. You intend to be gallant. You intend to have fun!

Which Tape Are You Playing?

Let's talk about an area where you should give serious consideration to making a change. Let's call it the Conversation Game. It's the art of talking *with*, not *to*--or *at*--, a woman.

There are two levels of conversation: there's the one men use among themselves, and the one they normally use when talking to a women.

Let's get past the usual lecturing, patronizing and male posturing. The challenge for men at this time is to take their worn out tapes and change them for a "higher vibe." This is a reverberating frequency, faster and more "present." It requires listening, really listening, to her. It requires tuning in and turning off your old, left-brain tapes. Getting yourself unstuck. It means losing the fear of rejection and jumping into the unknown. Scarier than hell! You bet, but the rewards--ah, the rewards. They're great!

When you talk with your buddies, it's probably about sports, your job, getting laid, working on your car, bike, whatever. The mistake a lot of men make is that they talk to women about the same things, except about getting laid. I don't know how to tell you this, but those topics of conversation are of zero interest to most women. Those topics of conversation are, for most women, boring.

When you first meet a woman, start talking to her. LISTEN to what she says, and turn on your newly acquired sense of intuition. You know what interests you, and if that's all you talk to her about, what are you going to learn about what interests her? This is where the game starts.

Put yourself in her place. This may be a lady you've known for years, or one you're meeting for the first time. She sees you. If she knows you, fine. If not, she sees you, likes what she sees, and finds you attractive. You're already ahead of the game. Then you walk over and start talking to her about the same stuff you talk to the guys about, and in that moment she tunes you out. She knows, automatically, that you're incapable of being interested or "present," because your male tape's running. One she's heard lots of times. You may be a nice guy, but she'll quickly realize that you're so totally involved in your own line of thinking that she'll tune you out. You've just dropped the ball in what could have been an interesting game.

Here's how you should play the game: *Intuit*. Please don't make this any harder than it is. How about having some fun! You see her. What's the setting? A street? The beach? A mall? On campus? An airport terminal? It doesn't matter. You are both occupying this same location at this same time, so you already have that in common. Lighten up!

You've seen her. She's seen you. Do not assume mutual attraction. If it is, great! You walk up to her, make a comment about the place. Nothing wrong with saying her hair is beautiful. The next 20 seconds are *crucial*, because women have a built-in radar for a guy who is only downloading his organic PC.

Can you communicate? Can you play the game as it should be played? With originality? With a degree of wit, intrigue? This is the crucial moment when you have to really focus on this lady's reactions! The perfect moment to exercise your newly acquired sense of intuition!

There's nothing wrong with asking for her help. You're looking for such-and-such. Does she know where it is? Do you have any idea of how amazing she's going to find it, that here is a man unafraid to ask a woman for directions?

I'm not going to write a script for you. I fully expect you to have the wit and charm to get the conversational ball rolling without any help from me. All I am trying to get across is, ask questions. Find out what she likes. Music is a good place to start. Is she into rock? Jazz? Classical? Country? If you find out that one thing about her, it will open a window into her interests. It will open a wide avenue of conversational possibilities. She likes classical, and you know nothing about it? Perfect! Ask her to tell you about it. Make it clear that you're willing to learn--from her. It's a two-way street. If you like a type of music she's not familiar with, then you become the teacher and guess what? You're learning about each other!

You've made it clear that you're interested in learning more about her and the things she likes. And she's learning that here is this nice man who is actually interested in learning about her and the things she likes. Don't you think that she might find that attractive?

At the beginning of any male/female relationship, right at the beginning, both parties send signals. If all he sees is a body he'd like to get into his bed, she'll know that. She'll know it because she's so used to seeing that signal. Ah. But what if he--or what if you--don't send that signal? Her response? Momentary confusion. What the hell is happening here? Then you begin talking, and you make perfectly normal conversation; and by doing that, you lower the threat level that she's used to dealing with. More confusion. And if you can actually find a way to ask for her help in finding something...are you getting the picture here, kiddo?

It's all a game. It should be fun, but most men don't know how to play it. They're over here talking BS that women don't give a shit about, and the ladies are over there wondering how come men are so dense.

This is a game to be played with all of the women in your life. Yes, it's great to have a new romance. However, there are many ladies among your family, friends, acquaintances who will welcome with open arms a man who really takes an interest in their lives. This is not a game to be used only for a romantic or sexual outcome. It is for *all* the women you know and care about, to show them your sincere interest as a loving man. This enriches the game! Raises it to a whole new level!

You wonder what women might want? One of the things any woman wants is your full attention--on her. She would like to think you're interested in getting to know her as a person. I can't stress strongly enough what an amazing impression that's going to make on her. On any woman.

Here is the secret: *Ask her questions*, and then truly *listen*. React honestly to her answers. Consider her a new course you're taking. One you're really excited to learn more about. How do you do that? You ask questions. You listen to the answers. It's like any game. In tennis you hit the ball. Then, if you're with a good player, she hits it back, and so on, and so on, and so on. Play with feeling! Ball zips back and forth. It's called conversation. Done well, it can be exciting as hell and a lot of fun! Done well it can also be very instructional. You'll both learn how to play the game better, this new game you're just starting. In Europe they call it flirtation!

Chapter 4

MENTAL FITNESS

Intention

I intend to release fear from my vibration

Working with Both of Your Heads

Woody Allen has said many clever things. Among these are: "My second favorite organ is my brain." Do I have to tell you what his first is? And what does that have to do with Mental Fitness? Actually...quite a bit. To be fit mentally means that you must learn to exercise control over what it is that's going on inside your mind. That you must learn how to perceive everyday realities in a way that you control them, and not the other way around. For example:

Erection. A uniquely male display. Sometimes they come when you least expect them. What's your reaction? Your mental reaction when that happens? Embarrassment? Probably. There you are, out in public, and then suddenly there "it" is, out in public. It doesn't matter what caused it. It's there, and you wish it wasn't. What's your response? Turn your back? Cross your legs? Anything to hide it, right?

Once upon a time there was this little boy. His Mom walked in and caught him beating on his erect little penis. "What are you doing?" Mommy asked.

"It won't go down!" the lad answered.

This being an enlightened Mommy, she smiled, sat beside her frustrated son, and gently explained to him that that part of him has a life of its own. That there would be times when it would get hard like that all by itself, and that should not bother him. There was nothing to be ashamed of. It was part of being a man. A part he would never have total control over. Very wise Mommy.

This is a subject that isn't discussed very much. It has to do with fathers dealing with their children. Without realizing it, children are extremely erotic. They have no discipline, no inhibitions. They climb all over you; they step on you and think nothing of it. The results of this innocent contact can sometimes lead to unexpected results. There is a lot of shame when this happens because men are so physical. Their being erotically turned on by this innocent play has nothing to do with the child. So what does daddy do? He decides that he's not going to have a certain kind of physical affection any more with his children. It isn't a total stopping of physical affection, but a stopping of a certain kind, the kind where his kids just roll all over him. Because he knows that he might get turned on, and it embarrasses him so badly that he stops that kind of contact. And this is very damaging, because it hurts both the child and the father in the long run.

How does it hurt the child? Remember, we're talking about a totally innocent being here. A creature in his or her most crucial formative years. A child who loves his parents, wants to show them the natural affection he's feeling. And even more important, he wants that affection back. He really needs it. Then all of a sudden, when he goes to play with daddy, he holds him off, and doesn't let him get close to him like he did before. What happens inside that child's mind? He senses rejection. And as the behavior continues, the child forms a perception: "I can't do certain things with daddy anymore. I can't show him how much I love him like I used to anymore."

The seed that's planted in a child faced with this type of rejection from his father is one that will continue a slow growth for the rest of his life. And when that little boy becomes a father and finds himself getting aroused when his kids press their little bodies up against him, the pattern will be repeated.

Why is there so much shame attached to a perfectly normal male reaction? Because there is great fear around the loss of control. Manhood and Control have, sadly, become synonymous in our culture. In truth, it's far more important to have compassion for yourself. The ability to take care of yourself with responsibility is a true sign of a man, one that begins with that man releasing shame.

Are you thinking about that--right now? Thinking about how you got turned on when you were dancing with sweet little Mary Lou that time at a school dance when you were twelve years old? How you sort of backed away from her so she wouldn't know? And how were you going to hide it when the music stopped?

The thing is, the music never stops. You are a man and you

have to begin the process of exercising control over both of your heads. Humor is a good place to start. Laughter is a great healer. Use your mind to stabilize, or to override the physical reaction with a smile, with a joke if necessary. Acknowledge that this is a part of being a man, and that an erection can be accepted as a masculine polarity. Please understand: what we're saying is to accept it for what it is, a natural male response. Nothing more. Nothing less.

Healing Wounds

Many boys are sexually abused. By their fathers, their mothers, male relatives, teachers, coaches, clergy. A relationship that was rooted in young trust is suddenly horribly violated, both sexually and emotionally. This hurt, this loss of control, the loss of their own selves devastates them and creates a barrier between them and normal loving relationships for the rest of their lives. Their wives, daughters, the women in their lives, will never know of this shadow on their spirit. They will speak of it to no one, and the wound will fester and never heal unless...

It wasn't your fault! Have compassion for the boy you once were. Stop blaming yourself if something like this happened to you when you were a child. This is crucial! It wasn't your fault! You were a child, an unmarked soul. And then someone you thought you could trust came along and soiled the purity that was you. Step back a second. See this through a third party's neutral eyes. Where does the blame lie? On the trusting child? Or on the adult who took advantage of that trust? No contest. If there is shame here, it belongs, 100%, to the adult. Yes, your innocence has been scarred, and yes, you can heal the mark. Here's how...

It all begins with forgiveness. First, forgive yourself. You did nothing wrong. You did nothing to be ashamed of, so begin the healing by understanding that most basic fact. It was not your fault! "I intend compassion and forgiveness!"

Next, and here comes the hard part. Forgive the person who violated you. There was a sickness in that person, an evil that he was powerless to control. Put yourself in his shoes for a moment. At some level, buried way deep inside, he knew he was doing something terrible and still he couldn't control himself. And the worst part was that he was doing this terrible thing to a child! To his son! To his blood relative! To his pupil! To someone he knew not only trusted him, but looked up to him, admired him! And he did it anyway because he was powerless not to do it.

A side note: In prison, the single most despised convict is the child molester. The other prisoners won't talk to him. Given the opportunity, they'll beat the shit out of him. Even society's outcasts hate a man who takes sexual advantage of a child.

"I intend forgiveness." Mine; the other person's. This is going to take a lot of effort on your part, but it will be worth it because until you begin the process of forgiving, there will always be a shadow on your soul. A coldness that will seriously affect your future relationships, especially with another partner. Whether it was a man or a woman who violated you, it will influence your life, and how you view commitment to another individual. Sadly, most of the time you won't realize the far-reaching effects of your youthful experience. "I intend to release guilt and shame!"

You know men like this. Let's call one of them Tony. He's got a good job. A nice car. His own home. But for whatever reason, Tony can't seem to commit to a long-term relationship with a woman. So what's wrong with Tony? Maybe he just wants to be "a player." Maybe he's immature. But maybe, just maybe, when Tony was a little boy, someone he trusted violated him, and because he's never been able to forgive himself, the shadow never went away.

Tony won't be attracted to long-term relationships. They imply vulnerability and permanence, conditions Tony feels he can't sustain. He feels a stigma forever attached to himself, a little sign that says, "I was violated when I was a little boy." His beliefs were trampled. What Tony prefers are casual relationships, often with unsuitable partners who are not permanent and do not imply the threat of vulnerability. Somewhere in the dark recesses of his mind, he's still blaming himself for what happened in his youth.

The intention to Forgive is one of the most powerful, one of the most liberating intentions you will ever practice. Whoever violated you, that shadow will remain a dark cloud that will affect your future relationships. Even worse, you might wonder if the wound you feel deep inside is somehow visible to others. Can they tell, just by looking at you, that a terrible thing once happened to you?

"I intend to forgive the person who did that to me." We said it wasn't going to be easy, but consider the purely selfish motive. Consider how much better, how much freer, you're going to feel when you pull it off. *It wasn't your fault!*

This freedom will allow you to do something you've never done before. It will allow you to talk about it. Not to publish a bulletin for general distribution, but to talk about it to the people nearest you. Your girlfriend. Your wife. Your best friend. Other family members. When you talk to your brothers and sisters, you might make an interesting discovery. They were molested too! How liberating is that going to be, for all of you?

"I intend stability." By intending that, you intend a reorganization of your inner self. You intend stability where before there was chaos. By forgiving, the inner turmoil will begin to ease. Light will touch your soul where before there had only been shadows. Stability will take its rightful place in your inner and outer life.

Stones Are Your Friends

Here's something you can do to help bring stability into your life, reduce stress, and make some powerful intentions.

Get some stones—small ones, smooth ones, some not so smooth; about eight should do it. Wash them in salt water, then set them aside. Let them absorb your atmosphere, and get used to you as you get used to them.

When you're ready to try the stones for the first time, lie face up on the floor—and you can do this with clothes on or off; it's up to you. Place one stone on your forehead, another on your neck, and one on your chest over your heart. Put one over each hip, one on each thigh, and a couple down by your feet. Then lie flat on your back for about half an hour and release tension in your body; feel it oozing out. Command your stress, and any other negative feelings, to leave your body.

Lie there and expel any negatives that are troubling you. "I intend to release unreasonable fears." "I intend to release anxiety." "I intend incredible relaxation." Make whatever intention you feel will best accomplish what this exercise is designed to do. Firmly believe that what you intend will happen, and then *allow* it to happen. And please, DO NOT worry about, "Am I doing it right?" That you are doing this at all means you're doing it right.

The first time you do this, since it is the first time, it's going to feel strange. I mean, here you are, lying flat on your back on the floor with a bunch of stones on various parts of your body. But once you're down there, take nice deep, slow breaths. Once you're aware of the stones, you can feel the ones near your stomach moving up and down with each breath. Once you start making your first intention, little by little the feeling of strangeness will begin slipping away. You are doing something totally natural, getting in touch with parts of yourself you may never have communicated with before, as the stones bring a deep earth frequency of calm and inner peace into your system.

After you've done this a few times, you'll feel totally comfortable with it. You will be totally comfortable with the concept of making intentions. You will begin understanding that it's perfectly okay to let your mind go wherever it wants to go. You may find yourself traveling to some interesting destinations. Don't fight it!

You may find your mind settling on something, or someone, that made you angry. Revenge is called for. It's a male thing, a control thing. It's perfectly natural until you learn how to do something about such negative, self-defeating impulses, impulses that imply that you're playing the Victim Game.

Observe this feeling of anger from a neutral position. Try to witness the event from outside of yourself. Was someone rude to you? Did something happen that you didn't think was fair? Were you the subject of an injustice?

Replay the event. Feel your anger. Understand where it came from and what, if anything, you think you can do to make it go away. And you can. "I intend forgiveness." Remember something: you're the only one feeling that knot in your gut when the rage comes back. The person who caused this anger is happily going about his or her business while you're working on an ulcer. "I intend forgiveness," and mean it. Let go! Continue your deep breaths; let the stones become a source of power for you. Let go! "I intend to ground my energy!"

While you're making intentions, and learning to release negative things, one of the most troublesome you can release is your fear of Rejection. It's been part of you since you were a kid. So many different ways life found to reject you. You didn't get picked for the team. That girl you asked out said no. The time you asked your dad for some help with a problem and he was too busy. And other major forms of rejection all along the way that haven't stopped yet.

While you're in this relaxed state, taking deep breaths, begin releasing your fear of rejection. You see a woman somewhere and you find her attractive. You'd love to walk over and say something to her, anything just to get a conversation going. But you don't. Fear of rejection stops you cold. Why? Think about this for a moment.

You see this interesting woman somewhere, and your first impulse is, I'd love to meet her. *Not* can I hit on her? A bit risky? Isn't it much more realistic to simply intend to talk to her? And much easier than to face the fear of "striking out?" Don't you think the rejection factor would drop considerably if that became your mind-set?

Have fun with this concept. The risk is not that great! Try it out. Nine times out of ten you'll be amazed with the results!

Fear is built into our survival instincts. It's perfectly natural, and indeed necessary to be afraid when we see an out of control car headed our way. The fear and adrenaline rush are what allow us to take the proper evasive action. And fear of losing a job will make us work harder. Fear is a terrific motivator, but only if it's *reasonable* fear. Our intention for this chapter is to release *unreasonable* fears from our lives, and you should have no difficulty knowing the difference.

By intending to release unreasonable fears from your life, your internal pressure will drop, and life will seem...well, less frightening.

Standing Naked in Front of a Mirror

I'm going to give you some exercises. We'll start with a really simple one, one that you might at first resist, and one you may find...unusual.

All that the first one requires is that you look into your eyes in the mirror, a good long look, and say, "I love you." Have you ever, even once, said that to yourself? There is a maxim that says, "If you don't love yourself, then nobody else will." Can't you see the blinding logic behind that statement? And this is a time when we must operate from a sense of the logic you're familiar with. In order to be lovable, you must first love yourself. Logical.

Put aside your feelings of embarrassment. And yes, I know it's going to feel funny the first time, the second time, the tenth time. Keep doing it, every day. Keep doing it until it feels less silly, and instead becomes true. Keep doing it until you're generating a good, healthy dose of self-love. You're a good person, certainly worthy of being loved, but it has to begin with you loving yourself. Please understand: we're talking about love, not conceit. Big difference.

You're doing this exercise to begin the understanding of yourself, of your true worth as a human being, as a male human being. You're not only accepting who and what you are, but truly loving that person. I really don't think you've spent a lot of time saying, "I love you" to yourself, but do it every day. Once you come to the point where you can look at your own reflection and feel love, trust me, you're going to feel entirely different, not only about yourself, but about everyone around you.

Once you're secure in self-love, and this is a process that will take time, you will find it amazingly simple to share that love with others, even with strangers. From even the briefest encounters, people you meet will sense that you like them, genuinely like them. And let me share a major truth with you. A woman who feels a man actually *likes* her, as opposed to just *wanting* her--she'll find such a man very attractive.

I'm not suggesting you do this next exercise right away. Take your time. Yes, this one is going to be a bit more difficult for some of you. It requires that you find a full-length mirror and stand naked in front of it. If you're a body builder, you've already spent hours and hours looking at your body in mirrors, so this will be easy for you. If you're in good physical shape, then doing this won't be so difficult, but if you're less than physically perfect--and gee, how many of us does that include? If you're less than physically perfect, you may have a hard time with this, but it's important that you do it anyway.

Begin by looking into your eyes. Focus on them and say, "I love you." Then go down to your shoulders, your chest; say, "I love you." I don't care if you're thin or overweight. Say it! Mean it! Continue down to your midsection, look at it, and say the words. Look at your genitals, "I love you." At your thighs, lower legs. "I love you."

It's possible that you're a man unhappy with his body, and you know why? Because it doesn't "measure up" to what society says it should look like. You've heard the stories about young girls who are already rail-thin going on diets because they think they're too fat. What is that all about? How stupid is that?

Just who the hell was it who was given the power to say which body shapes are "acceptable" and which are not? Well, no one was given that power! If you're unhappy with your body, it's only because you've been routinized to the point of believing there's something wrong with your physical appearance. That is pure, unadulterated bullshit! There is nothing wrong with you! There is nothing wrong with your body!

You stand in front of that mirror, look at your naked body and begin loving every square inch of it! If after doing this for a while, you feel you'd like to change your body--for you, not for anyone else--then you can do that. Being in good physical health is very important, and if adding a few pounds, or losing some, will get you there, go for it!

We talked about treating your body at least as well as you do your car. Give it regular maintenance, the proper fuel. If your car deserves that kind of care, don't you?

The whole point of the looking-in-the-mirror exercises is to get you to love yourself. To see and admire the amazing example of creation you are. No one is saying public opinion, style, fashions, don't have an impact on our lives, but they are, every single one of them, *other people's opinions.* The only opinion you should care about is yours.

Say Hello to Your Balls

Sound crazy? It's not. Here's what I want you to do: Think about how many different kinds of balls we chase. Balls of every size and shape. Round ones. Oblong ones. Big ones. Small ones. We chase after them with a dedicated passion. Well, how about giving your own balls the real love and interest they deserve? Do it! Astound yourself!

By learning to create magic, you'll bring back your intuition, restore your gut instincts. Go outside; take long, vigorous walks! Find some buddies; go fishing, and toss a football, or a baseball. Create a brotherhood based on *real* contact, not one based on the electronic numbing of the male spirit.

Doing this next exercise will increase the intensity of your orgasms, help you delay them for even greater pleasure. It will help you to do this because by strengthening your anal and sphincter muscles, you'll be able to contract them when you feel your orgasm coming, and hold it back, thus prolonging the intensity of your climax.

Look, I know this is out there for you, but that's the whole point. You're looking to make changes in your life, in your being, in your soul, in your mind, in your spirit! To change implies doing things differently. Accepting new theories. Practicing new disciplines. It implies opening your mind to new possibilities. Considering journeys beyond logic and ego.

It's as simple as looking at yourself in a mirror and saying "I love you," and as complex as accepting that self-love.

It all begins with you exercising your free will, and taking your first steps along this new path.

Testicle Breathing. This is a simplified version of a longer and more esoteric regimen that contemporary Taoist master Mantak Chia calls "the dance of the testes."

In their book, *ESO: How You and Your Lover Can Give Each Other Hours of Extended Sexual Orgasm,* Dr. Alan Brauer and Donna Brauer have a similar exercise labeled "testicle elevations." Testicle breathing directs energizing breath to the genitals, and helps to tighten and refresh the scrotum. Practicing daily also eventually leads to a man's being able to elevate and lower his testicles at will. Because the testes need to lift a little for ejaculation to take place, if a man is able to lower them voluntarily, he can delay his ejaculation while making love.

Make sure the room you are working in is comfortably warm, as you will be nude from the waist down. You can do this exercise sitting on the edge of a chair with your feet flat on the floor, and your genitals hanging freely. Or you can stand in a relaxed position with your feet apart, lower spine straight, and shoulders and neck slightly rounded. Focus your attention on your scrotum. Inhale slowly and deeply through your nose and visualize the breath going down and into your testes, filling them. As you do so, raise the testes. Exhale and lower your testicles. Imagine expelling negativity and accumulated toxins as you breathe out. Repeat this exercise nine times, then take a short rest. Do at least three, and up to six more sets of nine. At first you will find that you are engaging all kinds of muscles—anal, abdominal, PC— and probably will not discern much movement. The aim is to be able to visibly make the testes "dance" with as little muscular movement as possible.

Chapter 5

MAGIC

Intention

I intend all things are possible

There Are Doctors; Then There Are Doctors

Men have a tendency to rely on someone outside themselves to take care of their physical bodies. If something goes wrong, they go see a doctor. They're not as adventurous as women in the respect that they will not go to a doctor who practices alternative treatments, or someone who is not in the medical mainstream to take care of their problems. This is interesting in light of the fact that at one time men had to totally rely on themselves for their physical well being. What has happened to that once fiercely independent male spirit?

Most men in our culture have been conditioned to rely heavily on the use of the logical, left side of the brain. This is partly due to our western form of education. It makes sense in this context to use the most convenient, culturally accepted path for making life's decisions.

Could it be that men also look upon seeing those "outside" medical professionals as something only women do? Real men go to real doctors? Well, look around, guys. Some of the best physicians around are now beginning to accept non-traditional cures to heal very traditional problems. Their methods are far less invasive, and wherever possible, make use of the body's own healing powers. You might want to look into exploring this area of medicine the next time you have a physical problem.

Pendulums

Albert Einstein said that dowsing worked on electromagnetic forces. In this section we're going to introduce you to a power you have that you may not be aware of. Using pendulums. Here's how they work: You can hang one over a product you're thinking of buying, say in a market, and use it to find out if fruit is ripe. Which toothpaste is best for you, and so on. If it swings in the direction that says negative for you, don't buy it. If you have any food allergies, this is a skill you should develop.

Using a pendulum in public will require the exercise of your adventurous spirit. You will feel a bit strange doing that, but only the first few times. And think of all the interesting conversations this is going to lead to, especially with any woman who happens to be around. It's a simple thing to do, and it becomes extremely interesting to see the action when you stand in front of a rack of all kinds of different vitamins, shampoos, whatever. You get out your pendulum, and use it to see which one is actually going to work for you. And if none of them work, do some research on products; go to different stores.

If you're wondering where you can get a pendulum, relax, you can make one yourself. You can make it out of a simple old piece of crystal, or any kind of stone. Old crystal chandelier drops are a good source. Just put a chain, say between 8 and 10 inches long (could be less), attached to it so it can swing easily. Simplest thing in the world.

Here is where we put Dr. Einstein's theory to the test. The first thing you do is sit down. Hold it over your right knee and say to the pendulum, "Which direction is positive?" and it will either swing to the left or to the right. Some people are electro-magnetically set up so that their pendulum will swing left for "yes," and for others it will swing right for "yes." So you find out, number one, which you're set up for. And when you find out —say, it goes right for yes—that's your positive. And if it goes left, that's your negative. Now, if it swings in the middle that's neutral.

With time, anyone can work a pendulum—well, almost anyone. It will be a problem for anybody whose body is out of alignment, and also certain negative drugs will interfere as well. This is exactly the same mechanism used for generations by those gentlemen who use Y-shaped wooded branches to find water underground. They're doing the same thing, only their intention is to find water. So this is accessing your natural electromagnetic field, by which we are all surrounded, a field which is totally individual to you. It's like your DNA signature. Nobody else has your electromagnetic frequency.

We're electromagnetic beings. We have in us our specific fingerprints, our signatures. Whatever happened to you as a child and on into your adulthood—whatever age you are now--you have the imprints of all of the vibrational energies that touched and impacted your growth process.

For example: Why do you always attract the same type of individuals, male or female? Because there is an attraction force at work here. More specifically, your electromagnetic force. And you know what they say about magnets. Depending on the polarity, some attract, others repel. It's a basic law of nature, so you might want to consider becoming more aware of it.

Steps Along the Way

We're going to work through magic from different dimensions: spells, potencies, affirmations.

Step 1. THIS IS A MAJOR ONE!

Get your astrological chart done! Whether you realize it or not, you're connected to the stars, the planets, and to all of the electromagnetic energy that flows among them and around every living thing on this planet—which includes you.

It's worth your effort to find a good astrologer who will give you a truly accurate chart, one which begins with the moment you were born. Such a chart will help you a great deal in your life. It will give you your Tendencies. It will be very specific about the good and the bad influences around you, human or otherwise. You'll also find out what your Predilections are, and when someone who's qualified reads your chart, they'll be able to say, "Oh, this happened at such-and-such a time."

It's like having a master chart for yourself, which is why I'm recommending that you do this. If you truly want to experience the magic that you're capable of, you will need a first class astrological reading as a first step.

Dreams

You need to take more interest in your dreams. They are multidimensional, outside of time, and very intuitive, because they are not censored. Get a little book and write "Dreams" on the cover, and start writing them down. A small tape recorder also works, and will probably be easier. Here's what you can do:

When you wake up in the morning, lie there and keep your eyes closed so that you don't get fully awake, because that will immediately take you away from the dream state. Then remember as many of the details of your dream as you can—and no detail is too small to consider. Then either talk into the recorder or write it down. The important thing is to remember as much of your dream as you can before allowing yourself to awaken fully.

When you're made a few entries, listen to them, read them. You'll begin to notice patterns, themes that repeat. These are indications about your body—and about yourself. Quite often dreams are prophetic, and often quite practical as far as taking care of yourself is concerned. "Oh yeah, that dream means maybe I need to slow down, take a vacation."

Ultimately, you may begin having lucid dreams, where you wake up in your dream and actually face fears that normally you don't have to face in reality. This is one of the most interesting things you can do for yourself. One of the ways you begin getting in touch with your inner power, inner magic. Dreams can bend and move into whatever direction you choose.

If a tiger is running toward you in a dream, guess what? If you can wake up in your dream and say, "Ha, ha! I'm more powerful than you are, tiger! It's my game, not yours!" you will have taken a powerful step toward banishing a fear. Not of tigers, which you will probably not run into in your day-to-day life, but of what that tiger represents. With time, you'll be able to figure out what that fear is, and thus conquer it. Please understand that being able to make use of your dreams to come to a point of understanding, then interpreting them, will take time, but the results will be well worth your effort.

You can turn the tide in many ways. First of all, learning how to release fear. Magic and intention have a great deal to do with that, by allowing your mind to recognize what are basically vibrational situations, vibrations which carry your fears. These are the sum total of all of the vibrational energies that have piled up along your Life Path. It has taken all your lifetime to get where you are, so please don't expect change to occur overnight. You are embarking on a truly life-altering process here, and it is a process, so care enough to work at it. Be willing to give the effort that both it and you deserve. Desire and Will are two of the strongest motivators. Use them!

You're going to learn how to release fears, release any negative influences through a process called Visualization, which as the name implies, means imagining something in your mind's eye, or "feeling" something in your gut. This is about Transmutation. We're talking about dreams. We're talking about the electromagnetic system that surrounds you.

You will be given a series of exercises that will change you. But...to get that electromagnetic change in your system, you have to *will* yourself to change. You have to will yourself to be willing to change. Will yourself to be willing to work—because it *is* work. Work at the Transmutation of your spirit by playing the Intendo game, using your dreams, recording those dreams. All of these will be forces of change to your electromagnetic system, but without your Will and Desire to do these things, it won't work.

Another thing you can do in your dream state is incredible. Say you have a tough exam at school. Say you're working for a company and you have to make a huge presentation, or that you're faced with any task that's scary. Here's what you do: A few nights before whatever it is you're worried about is set to happen, when you go to bed—before you go to sleep, or as you slip into your dream state—you intend to play through the event and you *rehearse* it in your dream state. When you do this, you will have already done the event. So when it comes time to do the actual presentation, or test or whatever, it will have already been successfully completed by you in your dream state, and you will sail through it easily.

At the core of this is the fact that you have to do something you probably haven't done before. You have to believe that you are guided by your higher self. You intend to have *conscious awareness* of whatever the test or presentation is going to be, and to *know* that it will be effortless. When you actually have to do it, it will be as if you had done it before many times, which on another level you have. This is called working with the higher consciousness. Working with the higher dimensions

"I intend to take doubt away." Not, I "hope" to take doubt away. *Intend it!*

Becoming a Vibrational Magician!

"I intend safety, integrity and honor as I step into the un-known." It's worth reading twice. It's one more very important intention you should make when you go to bed. By doing that every night, you will increase your sense of stability, your sense of strength, because you will be reaffirming that you believe in yourself, that you believe that you are taken care of, that you are protected. You have the power to become a magician. You have the choice to transcend your current patterns. To affect your DNA by your thoughts and intentions.

By doing this, you are creating a probable future, which is what magic is really all about. Making dramatic changes in your future. Changes you intend!

You are now learning how to *create* your own future, not just living every day and blindly accepting events as they present themselves to you. And when you're creating your probable future, *wishful thinking is the key to creating your new reality, as long as it is grounded in practicality.*

All these years people have been telling you that wishful thinking is a waste of time. Wrong! You can bet the farm that most great inventions, most giant leaps forward in any field, came about because someone sat down and did some serious wishful thinking. You must first *imagine* before you can *create*.

We've already touched on how terribly routinized our lives are. While it may not be possible to fully escape from certain routine activities that our jobs, our lives, impose on us, your inner spirit can be liberated and allowed to soar. You are the only one with access to your thoughts, your imaginings—and yes, to your wishful thinking.

Without your realizing it, you have been hoodwinked out of your own divinity while being numbed down in a life of dreary routine. But…I have good news for you. Routine can be utilized. It can be made to work *for* you, not against you. By using your inner thoughts, you can fly wherever you'd like while doing any mind numbing work.

Let's take an Indian woman weaving a carpet. Same movements over and over, and yet while she's weaving, she can utilize the journey of the work itself to set her inner imaginings free, fly off anywhere she likes. You can do the same thing. CAUTION! We are not suggesting that you let your mind wander to the point where you ignore any of the basic safety guidelines of your job. If you're operating a piece of machinery, or any device with an inherent danger factor built-in, that has to come first.

What we are saying is that if you're trapped in a monotonous job at work, or at home, and it would be safe to let your mind take flight, then do it! Never forget: you can intend *anything* you like, *anywhere* you like.

Sexual Magic

I know that many of you have experienced the potency of a magical sexual encounter. Sexual magic is extremely important! Sex is the fountain of creation and power! Sexuality, in a committed relationship: it can be likened to space flight, because in a committed relationship, it can take you and your partner to other worlds. It's infinite ecstasy. It's not like anything else on this planet—not to mention that it's serious fun!

The place where this activity, this sacred event, usually takes place is in the bedroom. How does yours look? Is it clean? Is it cluttered with electronic gear? A TV? Your computer? A radio? Do you honestly think you're going to be able to take flights into the Infinite with all that electronic interference around? Sorry. It isn't going to happen. It all has to go, and I can hear you moaning already. "Take out my TV?" "Move my computer?" Well no, you don't have to do any of those things, unless of course you'd like a dramatic improvement in your sex life. It's your call.

If you're willing to make this change, here's what you should do after you lose the electronics: Buy some candles. Candlelight makes everything, and everybody, look and feel better. It's soft and warm, cozy and sexy. Go to a New Age store and ask for a smudge stick. American Indians used it; they made it out of sage and cedar. Smudge your bedroom. Send the smoke to every corner of the room. Smoke has magical and mystical powers. Don't ask yourself, "Why am I doing this?" Just do it. It's part of the changes you're making. Part of a ritual. Part of what's going to ease your journey into space. Intend that this room is set aside for the ultimate magical experience.

Intend to clear and clean the vibrational energies in your bedroom. By so doing you alter what had been there to what will be there. "I intend ecstatic orgasms!"

There is no other experience on this planet like sex in a sexually committed relationship. We have been given the greatest gift, one that leads to the formation of a new life!

This is an extraordinary experience that should be protected from all outside forces, including electronic ones. This is a loving and protected form of ecstasy, one that deserves, indeed demands, respect.

When you say, "I intend safety and honor and integrity as I step into the unknown," understand the words. You don't want anyone else to utilize this energy. And to keep it safe, you have to intend what it is you're going to do it for. The committed relationship is best because on that level you will create the most magical experience possible.

The opposite of a committed relationship is obviously an uncommitted one. The one where you casually scatter your seed all over the place. What's wrong with that? A lot. By being so careless, you will attract electromagnetic vibrations from all of your different partners. Liken this reckless behavior to a multilevel absorption of potentially negative energies.

This is a suggestion that will work wonderfully for a couple who want a child, or for any couple in a committed relationship. What I am saying is that the ultimate creative event is that event. It's the union of two people who truly love each other, cherish each other. A couple who have come together to experience a journey to a place where no one else will ever go because it's exclusively theirs.

This is a cosmic event they'll be sharing, co-joined, one spirit. They can travel to other planets, other places. The two of you can get together before the event. Smudge the room; light the candles; prepare your setting. Prepare yourselves for what lies ahead, then decide with intention where you'd like to go. "I intend a cosmic orgasm!"

One more time. This works best in a *committed relationship*, because that's the only one based on love. It will take the combined energy of the love the two of you share before you can journey to the stars and beyond.

Your Magic Wand

Yes—not just that one. It's used to summon and control spirits. We're talking about a real magic wand. You, as a man, are the seed of endless creation, and together with your Magic Wand, and with your magic, and with the coupling of a committed partner affirmed in trust and in love, you are part of the greatest force on this planet. So please understand: you are truly the source of creation.

The greatest highs come through the committed relationship, because it's based on love. Relationships outside of love can't possibly carry this power, and make no mistake, this is power we're talking about.

Chapter 6

THE GOLDEN BROTHERHOOD

Intention

I intend to awaken

There is a saying: "Power corrupts. Absolute power corrupts absolutely" Sadly, this maxim is rooted in truth. You have seen enough examples of this happening to know that it is true. It happens in all fields. Politics. Business. Sports. Science. The most basic questions now become, whose power? Whose reality?

When the Dead Sea Scrolls were found, they were jealously kept in the hands of a very select group of scholars, men who would let no one else look at what was on those ancient fragments of papyrus. It took almost 25 years before they would release the scrolls to the rest of the archeological community. Now, these were mostly good men, but they were seduced by the power that the scrolls gave them.

To one degree or another, there are negative forces at work out there. Forces which, if not guarded against, will turn us into something scary. One second Bob is the nicest guy in the world, then some idiot cuts him off in traffic and he goes ballistic. If he has a gun handy, Bob has been known to kill such vehicular offenders. This is not normal behavior. What the hell got into poor Bob? What possessed him to do that? Negative Forces?

"I intend safety, honor and integrity as I step into the unknown." This should become a mantra for you as you walk out your front door--every time you walk out your front door, or through any other door. By making the intention, you cloak yourself in a suit of armor, of protective, loving warmth.

You can deepen this connection by embracing nature. Get outside for God's sake! Feel the air around you. Hear the birds. Touch a leaf. Smell a flower. Sit up against a tree. Feel the Earth's heartbeat! The resonance of the sounds of nature will balance your brain by helping it resonate to the same harmony. It's all about frequencies—yours and everything that surrounds you.

"I intend to go beyond ego and logic." A major intention, guys. To go beyond ego, the self, to go beyond all of that! To truly go beyond logic. As men, we tend to be logical, orderly. It's part of our being so routinized. For you to intend to go beyond logic is a giant leap into a place you're not familiar with, and therefore not comfortable in. But you have to do it, because if you don't, you won't be able to accept the premise of why this book was written. To bring Magic into your life.

It might make it easier for you to take this step "beyond logic" if you redefine logic. Your present definition encompasses all of the logistical parameters you've grown up with, all you're used to. But what if there is an underlying logic or intelligence more basic than those? What if there are deeper natural and spiritual forces at work that you are simply not aware of? Does that mean they don't exist? Hardly. It simply means it's time you tuned to those other channels, the ones that surround you, and you are simply unaware of.

Begin by accepting that you are from the Sun. That you are a proud and vital member of the Golden Brotherhood.

Golden Brotherhood Breathing Exercise

Here is a simple exercise in breathing. Sit comfortably in a straight-backed chair, keeping your back as straight as possible, both feet on the floor, hands resting on your lap, palms up. Close your eyes; relax your jaw. When you're in this relaxed state, visualize a golden beam of sunlight. Focus that stream of golden spirals so it enters your body through the top of your head. Feel this golden, warm energy moving down through your neck, your upper body. Feel the warmth as it moves down through your solar plexus area, down to your stomach. Take your time; pay attention. You will recognize and feel the location in your body. You will become aware of the passage of this warmth as it flows downward through your body. Enjoy the sensation. You are doing this for yourself, and no one else.

Inhale from your gut, as you slowly count to seven, each count about one second apart, filling your lungs completely. Hold each breath for seven seconds, then exhale, again to the count of seven. Do this several times every morning and again at night. What are you doing? Several things. You're doing something you don't usually do. Concentrating on your breathing, becoming fully aware of the process, aware of the expansion of your lungs to their maximum capacity. Focus this golden light on your stomach, your feeling center. You can do this empowering exercise anywhere, any time.

Remember, direct the power of your father, the Sun, to enter your body through the top of your head, through your pineal gland, then down through your body, through your feet and down to the earth, as if it were a golden stream of energy. Focus on whatever part of yourself you like. Feel that you are grounding this golden light through you and into the earth. You begin by accepting this new magic and becoming aware of it. Then send the golden light through yourself from the earth back to the sun.

Bringing the golden stream into that place where gut instincts are formed, you are becoming aware of that place, aware of those possibilities, becoming more receptive to listening the next time one of them whispers to you.

This is one part of your new logic. Revitalizing a sensory gift you once had that has been lost because you simply haven't been using it. Use it or lose it, remember? "I intend the golden fire of the sun!"

You can do this breathing exercise throughout the day if you feel you need protection, increased awareness. Bring in the golden light, any time, any place. You can do it sitting in your office; you can do it sitting in a hotel room; you can do it sitting in your home. It's very simple. With practice, you will be able to send this golden energy to a loved one, and even to humanity at large!

Take five to ten minutes. Don't overdo it. You want to relax, and you want to bring in the Golden Brotherhood. You want to bring them in as protection and as your ultimate guardians, because as a member of the brotherhood, they will watch over you.

Death by Frequency

Entraining is a part of your old habits. It's what happens when you spend hours sitting in front of the TV or a computer. You become *entrained* to those frequencies, hooked on them because they're the only ones you're exposing yourself to. You do, after all, have other, far more productive choices. Move beyond that logic and into new, more creative pathways, pathways filled with frequencies that are beneficial to you.

I'm asking you to stop exposing yourself to harmful electronic frequencies that do absolutely nothing for you, and instead lock you into constrained bands of negative energy that suffocate free will and actions. These work against the empowerment of your spirit, while at the same time doing very bad things to your sex life! If men would only understand just how destructive this kind of continual exposure to negative electronic frequencies really are, they would stop that exposure, and the sales of Viagra would drop through the floor!

In the everyday working world, instead of making your life more difficult, remove yourself from an entrained society that is heavily into computers, information and left-brain activities, and you'll have an *advantage,* because you'll be able to intuit situations that other men will miss.

It doesn't matter what you do for a living. You can be an executive or a plumber, a bus driver, a school teacher or a laborer-- anything. Can't you see how being able to intuit a situation before it happens will be a huge advantage?!

This will take a huge leap of faith. We are moving from a data society to a perceptual one. The exercises you are learning here, practicing here, will help you make this crucial transition. Remember! Breathing in the Golden light, the deep breathing exercise, will stimulate your intuition and center your thoughts!

This is a beginning, a very important one. Before you can do something, you have to *believe* you can do it. Like I've been telling you all along, it takes effort, it takes work. Taking a detour off your Life Path onto a new one also takes courage simply because you're venturing into the unknown. But the payoffs will be huge!

You get a feeling, one you can't *logically* explain, and you act on it and you're right! Great feeling! You've plugged into something greater than yourself, but it IS yourself, your greater self, and everybody has one. But not everybody is willing to make the effort, expand the energy, to find that self. A self that is far truer, and yes, far more intelligent. "I intend clarity."

This is all about self-realization, and making the connection with your heart.

The ability to muster courage is a profound emotion, and men have too long been stunted by being told that real men don't show their emotions—to which I say bullshit! My god! It's so obvious! What could be a more masculine trait than being courageous! All we're doing here is using that courage to intend and direct our wills to doing things that take real guts!

For instance, let's go on a TV-Sports diet! How about taking a first small step by giving up watching all the non-local teams out there? You have no emotional investment in those teams, so how about not watching them?

It all gets back to taking steps to becoming the star of your own show. Make yourself the hero of your own games!

"I intend that I am a limitless being!" Stop placing an artificial ceiling on yourself, on what you are capable of. The only limits in your life are the self-imposed ones.

Let me remind you of a basic fact. You have a free will. You, and only you, decide what's going to happen in your life. You can decide to spend a glorious Sunday afternoon planted in front of the TV, or you can spend that same Sunday with your significant other, with your wife, with your children. You can watch a pro quarterback throw a football, or you can throw one yourself to your kids. It's your choice. Always has been, always will be.

This is a passionate, loving unconditional universe, and earth is the most beautiful living library. So use some common sense.

Go connect with the earth. Better yet, how about reconnecting? We live on this planet. We walk on its surface. We are surrounded by the astonishing beauty nature has freely given us, and what do we do? Ignore it. We have become so entrained, so unplugged from nature that we forget it's there.

Is it asking too much that you go out and spend a couple of days outside? Two nights sleeping on the earth? Two days inhaling what's around you? Connect with this place. Grab a handful of dirt; let it slip between your fingers, and as it does, imagine how long that dirt has been here.

Your body is composed of the stuff that was there when the universe was created! For a view of some of the rest, look up at the night sky and realize that what you're seeing happened millions of years ago, and the light from those events is only now, this very second, reaching us here on earth. At that moment, as you stand looking at the stars, understand your position as a visitor here, a very short term one.

Ask yourself, how do I want to spend the rest of my time here? It's your choice, remember? You can, if that's what you decide, go on doing exactly what you've been doing. Being part of the routinized mass that wakes up, goes to work, comes home, watches TV, and goes to sleep. Or you can choose to do something else. You can read these words, give them serious consideration, do the exercises, make strong positive intentions, and bring about a dramatic change in your life. "I intend stewardship of myself." "I intend stewardship of Mother Earth."

Gaining Control

This book, every word in it, has a single purpose. *To uplift the male spirit.* It's about showing you how you can bring magic into your life, providing you're willing to make the effort that it's going to require...providing you have the guts.

"I intend all things are possible." Okay, you just read those six words. Not good enough. They began with an *intention,* not a hope. You are not "hoping" all things are possible; you're intending. I "intend." Strong. Powerful. Leaves no room for doubt. "All things." All. Everything. Anything you want. "Are possible." Not "maybe." Not "perhaps." But ARE possible. "I intend that all things are possible."

To create and bring magic into your life you must leave room for the unexplainable and the unexpected. Use your mind and your emotional will to ask your guides, and the forces that are part of you, to help you become stronger.

Your greatest tool is your desire and your will through intentions. All you have to do is ask. Here I am in this world, living my life. I intend to enrich my existence. Today, right now, I am requesting guidance to help me _____. You fill in the blank. It can be anything you want help with. Your love life. Your job. Your family. Yourself.

"I am willing to do the work, to make the effort, to do whatever it takes to bring about those changes through whatever events or miracles are needed to bring those forces to work for me."

I don't need to know *how* those forces and miracles come together, only that they do, effortlessly, successfully, in a manner that satisfies my needs and intentions. Then you say thank you. Thank the forces for their help. "I intend gratitude."

This is playing the game, the game of Frequency. Ask for what you want, but don't ask *how* it happens. If you ask how, you are automatically out of the game. You don't wonder how electricity works, do you? It just does. Same applies here. Ask! Use your own magic and ask your guides to help you. Keep your intentions reasonable. Be ready for unexplainable and unexpected results.

Your power comes from your thoughts. From your sincere belief that what you intend is possible. You can add some significance to this exercise by doing something as simple as lighting a candle. Make a special place and center your thoughts. Create an area; add your stones. Add a crystal, some feathers, pictures that have special meaning for you. Use any artifacts to create for yourself a loving space, and then make your intention. That will isolate you in a tiny circle of light, shut out everything else, and help you focus and concentrate.

Say these words to stop the endless chatter bouncing around inside of your mind. "Take the doubt away." Say the words with resolve, conviction. Doubt weakens you, makes you indecisive. You want no part of it. Get it the hell out!

Don't just *think* it's going to happen; *know* it's going to happen. This is part of the ongoing exercise of your will, your free will.

This game needs balance and maturity, so intend that what you ask for is of the highest good. Then sit back, relax, and observe the forces at work. The unexpected will occur, so leave room for it, and be ready to accept it. Allow the spirits easy access to help you. Stay focused, and available for synchronistic happenings. These are seemingly chance events that occur simultaneously in one's life. These external events intrude upon our consciousness as we discover a connection, a symbolic meaning in our lives.

The most important faculty you need to begin developing is the strengthening of your will. Nothing is going to happen until you do that, because that's where all choices begin. You have to *choose* to change, and your will must be strong enough to not only ask for those changes, and believe they're going to happen, but be willing to accept them.

Listen To Me Yada, Yada, Yada...

There's something else men tend to do with each other. Lecture. They have this point, and by god they're going to get it out there! They do that with their male friends. With their girlfriends, wives. With their children. They lecture! "Here's what I think, and you're going to hear it!" They do this in all areas. You don't believe me? Listen to one of your buddies on the Monday morning after a football game. Listen to him lecture about all the dumb things the quarterback did. All the stupid moves the coach made. The same happens after any sports contest. He'll be happy to tell everyone all the mistakes every player made, every bad call the coach or manager made. Up on his soapbox lecturing!

When you lecture, it tends to shut down avenues for conversation. A lecture is, by definition, a monologue. You lecture your wife, and all she can do is stand there and listen, wishing your tongue would fall out so she could stomp on it. You lecture your kids, and they just tune you out. They're very good at doing that so you'll never notice.

What you might eventually notice is that you've lost the ability to communicate with the people you care the most about because you don't communicate with them. You lecture them, and who needs that crap? "I intend to listen."

As you begin practicing the Golden Light exercise, and begin opening yourself to accepting the intuitive messages that come from your gut, and acting on them, you'll find yourself becoming much more receptive to, and more sensitive to, the people around you. Especially the ones you care about. You'll be able to sense their feelings, their needs, and be able to do something about that. Helping them through moments of doubt, of fear, of uncertainty.

All it might take is for you to hug them. Just that one thing. Just that one simple expression that says, "It's okay. I understand. I'm here for you. I will listen to you."

You Have to be Willing

How many men feel that by having a superior intellect they already know it all, when in reality, what they have is a *congealed* brain. They are unwilling and unable to accept any radical new concept whose parameters are so far removed from the boundaries that they have unconsciously trapped themselves in. "I intend to create and open new realities in my mind."

Remember, we are stepping into uncharted territory. The place once spoken of with dread. Beyond this place lie dragons! Listen. Anytime you step into the unknown it's scary. So what? Does that mean you don't go there? Where would we be with that kind of closed-minded thinking? "Open new realities in my mind." God! Don't you find that exciting as hell! Come on, a little honesty here, just between you and me. Are you truly happy with who you are? Are you willing to accept the possibility of improvement? Take a moment to consider that. Are you happy with who you are? Are you *willing* to consider the *possibility* of improvement?

Steve McQueen died believing that he had never proved his manhood to his own satisfaction, or to anyone else's. How tragic is that? Here was this man who was the epitome of the rugged, supremely cool masculine hero, and he died unsure of who he was.

You don't have to do that. You can reach a point that Mr. McQueen never did. You can gain yourself. Gain yourself! You sit here, having read those words, and what's going through your mind?... "This is bullshit! I ain't gonna do this! It's a waste of my time!" Okay, good. Put this book down, toss it, get up and walk away. Done, over with!

That is old programming. Still reading? Still curious? A little curious? Hey, look. There are quite a few pages left. What do you think might be on them? Do you think that maybe, just maybe, on one of those pages are some words, a paragraph, a sentence even, that might make a dramatic difference in your life? Could happen, right? Shall we continue, you and I?

It has taken us thousands of years worth of conditioning to get to where we are. It has taken you a lifetime. If everything were okay, just fine. If society was humming right along with no problems. If there were no wars. If men and women were working as partners in perfect harmony. And if you were content with your life as it is right now, if you knew who you are, were aware of your own identity as a human being, this book wouldn't exist. There would be no need for it. Sadly, none of the above is the case.

Women aren't doing all that well either. They're angry because they aren't able to use their power, which is their role in the scheme of things. Co-creators of life. Bearer of children. The rock upon which the home is built and sustained.

We are going to ask you to do something. Not for me; for you. We are going to ask you to give yourself five seconds every morning and every evening, and at odd moments throughout the day, for a month. Five seconds. Pick an intention. Pick a specific thing you want to make stronger, better, and then intend it. "I intend greater creativity." "I intend greater wealth and comfort." "I intend success today in whatever I do." "I intend to be more sensitive to my family." It's your choice.

The selection process itself of what you're going to intend will begin preparing you, teaching you how to look at those areas of your life that you would like to improve upon. Get it down to one; then every morning and evening, as often as you can for one month, make that intention. Believe in it; believe in yourself; be willing and ready to accept the changes your intention will bring about. This is not something you share, not with anybody. This is for you, remember? This is an exercise of your free will. You are thus free to create any program you like as a gift to yourself.

Do not ask how. That lets in doubt. How this is going to happen doesn't matter. The how of it might come about through a totally unexpected channel. By asking you set limits; you narrow the possibilities down to those doorways you're used to. This is new territory you're exploring, so be open—to anything and everything. Never forget. You, as a man, were born an adventurer. Exploring is in your nature, but the last few thousand years have eroded that spirit, and taken it from you.

You, as an individual male, using the radiant power of your father the Sun, can begin taking that spirit back, providing—providing! you want to badly enough. Providing you have the courage to go there and bring it back!

"I intend to release the fear in my vibration."... I'm going to share another fact of life with you. Any negative force in your life is there because you cling to it, embrace it, hold it close. Any bad, negative, scary thing that ever happened to you exists only in your memory of that thing, that incident, that fear. The only way it can come back and re-enter your consciousness, is if you *bring* it back. Read that last intention again. "I intend to release fear from my vibration."

If right now you go back and remember something that made you feel bad, that scared you, that negative feeling will come back instantly because you invited it back into your mind. But what if you don't go back there, ever. Why would you even want to? Banish that fear, those fears, forever by never thinking about them again. And if something happened yesterday that frightened you, let it go. It was yesterday, history.

To be afraid is part of being alive. Scary shit happens. But it can only hang around as long as you allow it to hang around. "I intend to release fear from my vibration." The more you think about it, and see how obvious it is, the easier it will be for you to release fear from your life.

Who Owns You?

Earlier we talked about your electromagnetic field, how it's uniquely yours. I imagine now you give that topic much more thought as you move through the course of a day than you did before. What am I attracting? How can I protect myself? How about, "I intend safety and protection."

If you don't protect yourself, someone, or something else, might move in and claim a piece of you. If you ignore your field, your electromagnetic property, or are careless with it, bad things can happen. Bad things are happening. Stay aware!

By losing even a tiny piece of your field, you lose more than a tiny piece of yourself. "I intend awareness."

By being careless, others can take control of that tiny piece and begin exerting outside influences that are not in your best interest. They can begin making subtle changes in your true nature, perverting it. Think for a moment. Think back to an incident, a recent one, when you did something that you later felt was totally out of character for you. Did you lose your temper? Did you shout at someone you never thought you'd shout at? Do something you never thought you were capable of doing? If something like that has happened, and for that brief moment you weren't in control, then who or what was?

"I intend that I am not available for any outside being." By intending that, you are expressing an awareness of your electromagnetic field, putting a wall around it, protecting it, and you, from any and all outside influences. This is all about becoming conscious, more aware.

Your image of your reality is another subject we've touched on, and I can give you a great example of that. Did you see the film entitled *The Truman Show,* with Jim Carey? In it, his every move since the day he was born was a live television program. His world was an elaborate set, and everyone he met in that world was an actor, including his parents. Everyone knew this was a show—everyone, that is, except Truman. His life, his totally fabricated life, was his reality...until the day he bumped up against a horizon and found it was a painted backdrop.

What's your reality? Are you an actor in someone else's show? No? Are you sure? Anytime you give yourself over and become a spectator to someone else's show, you become an actor in that show. You hand over your life, for however long his show lasts, to him. You cheer for him, whistle and applaud for him. You urge him on. So who's cheering for you? Who's urging you on? Who's rooting for you? Do you see anybody doing that?

What's your reality; who are you, really? Who is writing your story? Yes, it's great when the home team wins, but...that's their victory, not yours. How much satisfaction can you get from someone else's winning effort? None. Ah, but what if the effort was yours? Then what? It doesn't have to involve an athletic contest, although getting with some of your buddies and playing a game, any game, and winning—well, that sure beats watching somebody else win, by a landslide!

You can capture this same terrific feeling of achievement all by yourself. You can do something you've been saying you were going to do for months, but never got around to. Wax the car. Clean the basement. Put your tools in order. Do that thing, whatever it is, that you've been putting off, and when you finish, sit back, relax, and let the feeling of accomplishment wash over you like a nice, refreshing wave. You did it! YOU! You finally got around to doing something you've been saying you were going to do! Hey! You might actually get some applause!

There is a flip side to feeling good when the home team wins. How you feel when they lose. Gloom. Your whole day's ruined. Maybe even your whole week. But wait a minute. It's not *your* defeat. They lost, not you. You had no more to do with their losing than you did with their winning.

ENOUGH! Bring in the golden power of the Sun! Let it flow through you, over you, in you. Reconnect with your limitless energy source so that you can play the part of a powerful being through your heart! Become the star of your own show! Become the hero of your own game! Stop cheering for the other guy, for men you don't even know, and who don't know you exist, and start cheering for yourself!

"I intend that I am a limitless being!" No limits! None!

By connecting to the Sun, you will begin activating your brain, your heart, your too-long-dormant gut instincts! Where before there was doubt, shadows, now there will be certainty, and light. Don't forget, "Take the doubt away!"

If you don't believe in you, who will? If you can't believe in the nobility of your male spirit, who will? And the male spirit truly is noble. Left to follow its natural course, it is loving, protective, adventurous. Sadly, that natural course, that intended flow, has been detoured.

Forces over which the male has no control have, for many decades, corrupted his spirit, his soul, his heart; and look at the results. Chaos. Confusion. Anger.

I want to talk about anger for a moment because it has become so pervasive, among both men and women. There are terms that have entered our vocabulary that didn't exist just a few years ago. *Road Rage. Sky Rage. Sideline Rage.* Rage and more rage. Where is it coming from? What causes it?

The American Automobile Association actually has a name for a particular type of rage: *Mad Driver Disease.* A symptom that rose 7% every year during the 90s!

Airlines, especially cabin attendants, find themselves having to deal with passengers who are completely out of control with rage. People whose friends are astonished to hear of their outbursts because back home, "Gee, Fred's the nicest guy you'd ever want to meet."

And in one particularly horrible incident, a father angered over rough play in his son's hockey game beat another father to death! What the hell is going on here? Where's all this anger, this rage, coming from? Doctors will tell you that the average male does not get enough rest or sleep. These sleeping patterns are so disturbed that they have become a major factor in their health and longevity. Women live longer. One reason: they have better sleep patterns.

Americans spend more time working than anyone else in the world. Up until a few years ago, when we left work, we left it, but not anymore. Now we have cell phones. Now we can be reached 24/7/365. No escape. Someone can call and upset us while we're humming along at 70 miles an hour on the Interstate. I hope I'm not in the car in front of you when you get one of those calls.

The technology that was supposed to make our lives easier has done so, but at a price. Where once upon a time an incorrect keystroke just meant going back and fixing it, now the simplest mistake on a computer can cost millions, throw a production line into chaos, or upset markets around the world...all of which brings us to...

Tension. Self-imposed or work related, it's always there. The productivity standards seem to keep increasing, but you still have only the traditional eight hours to get them done. More is expected, but rarely appreciated. And then after a killer day at work you come home, and someone in your family makes the most innocent request: "Daddy? Can you fix my bike?" "Sweetheart? Can you change the bulb in the garage?" You can't, not at that moment; you are not capable of doing even one more thing. Melt down.

But what if while you were at work you said to yourself, "I intend serenity." What if while you were driving home you said to yourself, "I intend serenity." Would doing that make all the BS go away? No, but it would reduce its negative impact on you.

When that careless, rude, talking-on-his-cell-phone-while-cutting-you-off-in-his-BMW gentleman zips by-- "I intend serenity." You can say it out loud, maybe even yell it at him. It will probably make you laugh, which sure as hell beats screaming obscenities at the top of your lungs and accelerating with the intention of running him off the road.

You can do that or...you can keep replaying the incident in your mind, in your free will, while bringing back the anger over and over. Strong emotions are much easier to recall, and this surely fits into category. So a week later when you see another BMW, you can remember, and get your stomach in an uproar all over again—and isn't that doing you a lot of good?

Relax. You don't have to get this in one sitting. Your life has been an evolutionary process, and so is this. All we're doing is talking about using your will in ways you never have used it before. This isn't a foreign language we're asking you to learn; it's simply a new way of perceiving your life, yourself. It's about taking control--one of your favorite words--of taking real *control* of your surroundings. It's about creating games where you can be the hero, the star player.

This is a new skill you're learning, and like any new skill, to be good at it you have to practice. By learning how to direct your will, your free will, you will be able to venture, for the very first time, beyond your ego, beyond your logical mind. Those negative influences we mentioned have conspired to congeal your brain, lock it down, and narrow its potential to the point where new ideas, new philosophies are kept out. Too dangerous! Too radical! "My God, Orville! You and Wilbur actually think you can make that thing lift off the ground and fly?"

Earlier we talked about "rehearsing" a future event in your dreams so that when the real thing actualiy happens, you won't be afraid, or feel any anxiety, because is your mind you've already not only done that thing, you've succeeded in doing it. There's another thing you can program yourself to do that has to do with anger, rage and forgiveness.

Release the Past

Let's assume you're angry with someone—anyone—and it's eating at you. Wherever you happen to be, relax; let go of the negative feelings by saying, "I intend to release you (name) in peace." You can even do that with the BMW guy. Just let go of the anger. LET GO! It's in your power to do that. By releasing the person, you also release yourself. By releasing the rage, you banish it from your mind, from your memory.

By making the intention and meaning it, the corrosive revenge factor will fade, disappear. This is you we're working on, not somebody else.

There's another intention you can use that will help you tremendously with unresolved relationships, especially those having to do with your family. "(Name), I bless you and I release you in peace. I release you to your highest good." Look at what you've just intended. Your blessing, and that whoever the person is, you release him to his highest good. An intention filled with your love and most sincere good wishes for that person with whom you're having a problem. If you say that, and truly mean it, you'll immediately feel lighter, less burdened, at peace.

What we've been talking about are situations where you've allowed others to exercise strong, negative influences on you through their invasion of your electromagnetic field. That's why the more protective you become of that field, the more difficult it will be for anything or anybody to invade it. Are you getting the picture? Be able to say, "I intend that I'm not available," and mean it.

You've come this far with me. Far more important, you've come this far with yourself. That tells me that you're at least willing to accept new concepts, new ways of thinking, new philosophies that until you picked up this book were some you didn't know existed. That's all well and good, but if all you do is read and not act, then you're wasting your time--the most precious, most valuable, and most limited of all of Life's commodities.

To go beyond your ego is to step past a threshold you're totally comfortable with and into unexplored territory. We've used the word scary to describe that passage. We've also used the word adventuresome to describe the male spirit.

By venturing beyond your ego and the old form of logic, you'll be taking a step forward. You'll be entering a higher level of awareness that's always been there, waiting for you to come and visit. A place some women are so comfortable in, that place where their famous Female Intuition resides.

There is nothing to be afraid of! You're not being asked to jump from a plane and pray that your parachute opens. These are baby steps you're taking. Make intentions. Scary? Hardly.

Sit in a chair and bring the golden stream of the Sun into your body. Scary? No. Start creating games that star you. Scary? I don't think so.

Once you do get past your ego, your notoriously fragile male ego, you'll finally be able to ask for something you desperately need but have always been afraid to ask for. Your ongoing fear of rejection has kept you from making this utterly simple, most basic request:

"I need your love." Four words that upon hearing them, will melt a woman's heart. Four words that upon your saying them, will break down a barrier that has for all these years kept you from experiencing true love.

By simply admitting your need, you've taken a giant step beyond your ego. You've done this by admitting you need something "real men" never admit to: that you need love. If for one second you doubt the power of uttering those words to the woman in your life, or to your family, your children, imagine them saying those words to you. To hear that your love is needed by someone you care for creates a great rush of protective energy and an instant outpouring of your love. It takes great courage to admit you need something, or someone.

So what do you think? Are you willing to exercise your free will and begin doing these things? These utterly simple, non-scary things?

It begins with courage. Imagine yourself walking into a bookstore, and you have no idea what kind of book you're looking for. You walk along the aisles and you're surrounded with choices. Now what? You use your new awareness to select, make choices--your choices; but always leave room for the unexpected. You did that when you got this book. You chose it from among many other possibilities. You did that because at some level you were open to exploring new realms. Open to accepting that there is an untapped universal energy out there that might just help you to realize your full potential.

We just said how much courage it takes, especially for a man, to admit he "needs" something. It took a degree of guts for you to buy this book, because by doing that, you admitted a need. That is not a sign of weakness. Quite the contrary. The man who can't admit he needs something is usually operating from fear, from the typical macho posture that says, "I'm just fine. I don't need any help."

Chapter 7

GOLDEN LIGHT EXERCISE

Intention

I intend an open heart

We've talked quite a bit about bringing the power and energy of the Sun down through the top of your head and into your body. Now take your next gigantic leap into this "unknown" and intend, before you start, that you are safe, protected and honored as you take this step.

As you know, it begins with you finding a quiet time. I know that for some of you this may be hard, but somewhere, someplace in your home you can do this. You have already set up an area that has your stones, etc. To help isolate yourself from what normally surrounds you, light a single candle and sit in a comfortable, straight-backed chair with your spine erect, feet firmly on the floor. Rest your hands on your lap, palms up, and close your eyes; begin visualizing a stream of golden sunlight coming down and through the top of your head. Imagine it in the form of golden spirals swirling down. Relax. Relax everything: your jaw muscles, your tongue. Roll your eyes back, relax your shoulders, and so on down throughout your entire body. Feel deeply, deeply relaxed, eyes closed. Feel the energy of the sunlight moving down through your body, flowing through your heart and your bones, through your fibers, your organs, your cells, warming them, warming you with the love of the sun. Feel every strand of DNA in your body glowing with this golden energy.

When you reach this state, which should only take a couple of minutes, begin the seven second count of inhaling; hold for three, then again a seven-second count as you slowly exhale. Do this by breathing deeply from your abdomen, and fill your lungs to their capacity while you exhale.

Now become aware of the energy of the sunlight coursing through your bloodstream, being pumped through your heart, warming it as it floods your entire body with that gentle, soothing warmth. Taking deep breaths in, holding, slowly exhaling. In...hold...out. Feel the air passing through your nostrils, becoming fully aware of its passage in and out. Feel the Golden Light filling your lungs. A deep, rhythmic intake of air from the bottom of your stomach and then releasing it.

Feel your heart expanding, with your lungs and solar plexus relaxing. Feel the Golden Light fill every cell in your body, infusing it with this vibrant, golden energy. *Your* energy. A gift from your father the Sun. Visualize this happening! Feel it!

As you do this exercise, do so by bringing in whatever geometrical symbols best inspire you.

"I intend rejuvenation and regeneration," and believe it. What you're doing here is creating a powerful, natural link by making an intention through your mind to your heart, and to your entire body.

This is a game of imagining, so it won't make any difference if you feel anything the first few times. But by simply doing this exercise, you're taking another step beyond your logical mind. You're doing this by making a commitment to do an exercise that doesn't seem, at first, logical.

It will help a lot if you can concentrate, if you can visualize that stream of golden energy coming down through the top of your head, feel it going through your body. The stronger your level of concentration, the clearer your visualization, the sooner you will reach a level where you will begin feeling the energy, the warmth.

A point will come when you will see or feel the flow of this golden energy moving in a figure 8 through your brain. The figure 8 starts in the center. Go to the top center of your head and go in two inches. That is the pineal gland. The flow will start on the left side, move through your pineal gland in the center, then around to the right side. You then arc that energy out through the top of your head, down to the base of your spine, up your spine and up to your brain again. Do two things at once: keep the circle 8 moving and arcing down on the outside of your spine, connecting with your tailbone. Then bringing that arcing beam up through your spine and back up into your brain. Keep repeating the sequence.

This is a symmetrical course that you will repeat again and again, spinning it slowly. And as you're spinning it, you will allow yourself to see the sun. To see the sun from a distance. See it as a direct point from your forehead center to the sun. Your eyes remain closed. And you'll see yourself standing out on a beautiful landscape. A landscape of a desert, but a desert that has all of the beautiful flowers of spring. And you are, from a very great distance, watching the sun. You're looking at the sun, but it is not hurting your eyes to bring in the light of that sun through the center of your forehead, and the top of your head itself, and see it from both places. And as you stand there, you're going to see in the distance the beautiful sunset of an absolutely gorgeous day that is ending.

And as you watch that setting Sun, you will feel the depth of the golden spirals coming in, and at the same time you'll be feeling that great golden light spinning and hitting the inside of your head as the figure 8 moves through your pineal gland, arcing down and up your spine. As the Sun goes down, you'll see the true beauty of this planet, and you're going to be in two places at one time: sitting quietly in your chair and standing in the desert. Then suddenly you'll see a huge flash of light. Then you can come back into yourself...slowly...slowly. And then open your eyes. "I intend divine nonchalance." Now you'll be in a relaxed, casual, ready-for-anything state of mind.

DO NOT put pressure on yourself! DO NOT raise your level of expectation! The whole idea here is to r-e-l-a-x. Let the golden stream flow through your body as you deeply breathe in and out. In this state you can travel anywhere, here or in the cosmos, by bringing in the intelligence of the sun! Put no limits on your imagination. And journey anywhere!

By doing just that for, say, three to five minutes, it will certainly help you relax, and take you away, if only for a moment, from the world you left behind. And when you go back to that world, you'll see it through different eyes. And remember, the fuel for this exercise is love. Unconditional love!

Observing Is Good

You walk into a restaurant, the kind where reservations are not required, and you have to wait because it's busy. Instant tension. You feel it. The lady with you feels it. Finally you get seated, and your harried waitress comes over and hands you menus. You can tell that she's stressed, so you look at her and say, "It's okay. We're not in a hurry." You'll see the tension drain from her face, replaced by a smile. You've just become her favorite customers.

By becoming more sensitive to the people around, you will know how best to deal with them in ways that lower the stress and tension levels. The next time you're...anywhere, and it's busy, get the eye of the person trying his or her best to cope with the insanity, the one saying, "I'll be right with you!" Then say the magic words, "I'm not in a hurry," and watch what happens.

Increased sensitivity will work wonders for you throughout the course of your day, and your life, and it takes such little effort to improve yours. Observe, feel, sense, react.

To Observe is just that. Observe the situation. Gauge the stress level.

To Feel is the ability to put yourself in the place of the people trying to cope with the chaos.

To Sense is to understand what they must be feeling.

To Act is to say or do something to ease the pressure.

Now, if when entering this situation—no matter where it is, including if it's in your home—and you bring added tension with you, things are only going to get worse.

This is all about you getting to know you better. It's about you getting more in touch with your feelings, and the feelings of others. This will happen as you continue the exercise of bringing the stream of Golden Light through your body, feeling it flow through your body, your blood, your organs. This will bring vitality to your body, and will stimulate your mental activity as well.

Don't expect miracles. This is a divine new talent you're developing. It's going to take time. It's going to take faith and your sincere belief that, little by little, you will increase your sensitivity and your long dormant sense of intuition. Self-awareness will come first; then gradually you will become more sensitive to others around you. It's important that you firmly believe this every time you sit down and bring the radiant, energy-filled light of the Sun down through your body. This simple five minute exercise has the power to truly bring magic into your life and change it, forever.

By simply living on this planet we expose ourselves to danger on a daily basis. Think back. When was the last time you were in a dangerous situation? When was the last time you felt uncomfortable, and felt powerless to do anything about it? A terrible feeling, wasn't it? The next time such an event happens, here's what you do:

As you become more sensitive, you'll start becoming aware of dangerous situations as they develop. If you have a gut feeling that something bad is about to go down, get the hell out of there! NEVER question a gut instinct! That part of you will never lie.

If flight is not an option, here's what you do: Feel the rush of golden light coming down, and use it to create an egg-like protective shield around yourself. Feel like you are in a large oval. This is not a fragile, drop-it-and-it-cracks egg, but rather a shell that will protect you. It can be a crystalline structure, or any other structure your imagination comes up with. Forming it takes the blink of an eye. You will it to happen, and it happens.

Once it's in place around you, fill it with anything you like. Fill it with something that will cushion you--with rose petals, balloons; it doesn't matter. Fill it so that it fits comfortably around you, with you inside it. This also happens quickly. See that crystalline structure as solid as a rock that nothing can get through. Nothing. When you have that protection in place, you must use your will and your strength! "I intend safety!"

Red Rock

Are you ready for a really multidimensional leap? Okay, then listen to me. We're in the process of expanding your realities. We're in the process of doing that by first letting you see what your current reality is. It has to begin there, and we've already gotten into that.

Part of your new reality is your acceptance of thoughts, of concepts, philosophies, possibilities. Of exercises, results, sensations and awarenesses you were previously unaware of. The existence of other dimensions is one of those new concepts. Can you accept that possibility? "I intend a multidimensional reality!"

Good. Now back to Red Rock. Pay attention. This is a powerful thought-form you can access anytime you feel in danger or threatened. You can also use it to protect others as well. This is a thought form held by a group-mind that affords protection and balance. Red Rock is a command that activates energy protection. A vortex of healing and invisibility, it absorbs and cushions distorted vibrations.

By evoking Red Rock, you'll be calling upon a power that is outside the three dimensions you're so comfortable with. And the minute you start asking how that is possible, that's the minute it becomes impossible. You can Red Rock your home, your family, friends, business, etc. Just ask, and invoke the words, "I Red Rock myself today." Use your imagination freely on this one. It's very powerful, and used in conjunction with your will, can create a magical force. This is a loving manifestation of your intelligence. Use it wisely!

Energy Fields

There are people who, by simply entering a room, charge it with energy. The common term for this is "charisma." It's hard to define, but when someone has it, everyone around him notices. That is part of that person's aura. It's also part of his singular electromagnetic field that is generated by his frequency.

We are, every second, bombarded by frequencies. Some we can do nothing about, like the frequencies that rain down on us from the atmosphere our planet is orbiting through. The frequencies generated by every electronic device we come anywhere near. And all of these outside frequencies have varying degrees of impact on our own inner frequency, that electromagnetic resonance that is uniquely ours.

Then there are those other frequencies we're exposed to that we do have total control over. Primarily the ones radiating from your TV set, computers, cell phones, etc. We happily invite those into our lives on not only a daily basis, but also on a prolonged basis. Not a good thing.

We talked about this before, so this is only a reminder. The term we used to describe the negative impact on the brain of constant TV viewing was *flatline*. Such exposure tends to numb the brain, in effect rendering it partially dead.

There is no intellectual activity required to sit and watch a television show. As you're doing that, you turn your intellect over to someone else, to mindless images you had no part in creating. This is the ultimate machine for mind control. Electronic frequencies create havoc with your nervous system.

I'd like you to expand your natural powers. Here is an amazing exercise that will help you do that. If you can manage to get hold of pictures of yourself when you were a child—say, when you were five years old—another when you were 12, and others taken as you grew, look at them. Not as you always have, but with your new, more perceptive eye. Can you notice subtle changes in that face? In the body language? Is the person in those pictures becoming more or less assertive? Expansive or shy? Can you sense the growth of his aura, or has it diminished?

How has Life treated that kid? And how is the adult man doing? Is he energized, vital? Or sad and defeated? Life can do terrible things to us. Change us in ways that leave scars but...but we can heal those wounds, heal ourselves. In fact, we can go back to the time when those wounds were inflicted. We can alter our past. We can change; we can reinterpret what we thought happened to us back then.

So let's go back. Let's go back to any painful incident in your life. It can be anything, but an event traumatic enough that it left a mark on your soul you've never forgotten. A hurt that doesn't go away. In that moment, because of that incident, you saw your-self as a victim. Someone took advantage of you, and you've never gotten over it. The trick is to look at that child or man, and using magic with clarity, you can change your past by removing the pain from your electromagnetic field. This is the beginning of reinterpreting what happened to you in your past, and can be a major opening for the forgiveness that will bring you peace and completion.

You remember when we talked about young boys being abused? The terrible, never-healing wound that kind of thing leaves behind? We talked about how crucial forgiveness is in getting past that painful memory.

Sitting here now, think about something terrible that hap-pened in your past, and how badly it made you feel. What a damaging blow it was to your self-esteem.

Do your best to closely examine the event from all sides. From yours, and from the perspective of the other person or persons involved. If doing this causes you pain or discomfort, it's okay. That's part of the process of altering your past for a more harmonious and pain-free present.

Begin by manifesting a non-victim image of yourself. Mani-fest your past with imagination and will from a position of dis-passionate love, so it will be those two elements working to-gether to create a new point of view. It's by intending to do this, to go back and alter one interpretation and replace it with another that doesn't hurt, that you'll be able to ease the pain and let it fade away.

See the person who injured you through this fresh point of view. Visualize what motivated him to do what he did. Was this a deliberate act of youthful cruelty? Was revenge involved? Was it racially motivated? Sexually motivated? Whatever the reason, while you may not know what caused the outrageous behavior, you do have the power to change your view of the outcome.

Okay. You've got the memory; you feel the pain. But now you've got something you never had before. You've got the "current you" visiting the past, and looking at it through adult eyes and the clearer perspective that only time brings.

Your job is to forgive those who injured you, whether those wounds were real or perceived. Ask your ancestors to change their DNA codes, along with yours. Reach into your past and inspire and correct any painful memories as you create this new interpretation

There are three of you now: the past you, the present you, and the future you, the you who will no longer be burdened by a memory that has haunted you long enough. By doing this simple exercise, you will have changed your past, your image of yourself as a boy, and that of yourself as a man. No more remorse. No more guilt. No more self-pity.

You'll be able to do this because moving back and forth between your past and present is nothing more than an elimination of the time barrier, and a part of multidimensional living. It's another part of your journey beyond logic. That boy is just fine. So is the young man, and so are you. Become that incredible, brave male warrior guardian that our planet so desperately needs right now!

How to Manifest

We began this by talking about charisma, how you can acquire your own brand of that marvelous aura. Let's see how that works: Through intending manifestation you can alter your past. You have the ability to change your image of a past reality, and reality is what this is all about. *Your* image of *your* reality! An image you have total control over. And there's the "C" word again. It's there because if you *don't* have control over your own reality, you have a serious problem.

You can alter your present reality by simply manifesting the changes you'd like to make. By bringing those changes to life.

It always begins with the basics. What is it about yourself you'd like to change? Do you wish you were a better dancer? Take lessons—great place to meet women, by the way. Do you wish you had a better personality? What's wrong with the one you have? Seriously. What do you think is wrong with it? Too shy? See if there's a chapter of the Toastmasters of America in your town, and if there is, join it. They'll teach you how to be comfortable speaking in front of people. And once you can do that, which is considered one of the most frightening things a person can do, the rest will be easier.

Do you wish you had a different body shape? Go to a gym to bulk up; it's also a good place to meet ladies. Exercise and change your eating habits to lose weight. Both will require a strong dedication on your part, but aren't you worth it?

Whatever you think is wrong with your personality has a solution. If you want to change it badly enough, you can change it! And if you don't care enough to even try, then accept who you are and stop complaining about it!

Consider yourself a "work in progress," this new being you're going to create. As you move forward, your self-confidence will grow. Your self-image will change. People will notice. They will see you differently. And what they will also notice is . . . your charisma! Those pulsating frequencies that now surround you! That great electromagnetic energy flooding your aura!

Now that you better understand and appreciate the power of your mind, your intellect, and your imagination, how about starting to exercise them?

We've barely touched the surface of what manifesting can do. This is a very powerful concept you're adding to your arsenal of tools that has the ability to alter the course of your life.

To manifest simply means to bring to life. You can manifest anything, providing you believe that you can, and that you are willing to make the conscious effort required.

First you have the desire, then the will, then the divine nonchalance to watch the outcome.

#1. See a clear image of what it is you intend to manifest. Work on that until you can visualize every detail of that thing, of that abundance. Reality must be a part of this. If you visualize yourself as being richer than Bill Gates, that's not realistic. But intending wealth is realistic, providing...you know the rest. "I intend to be comfortable with wealth."

Manifest your intention. Believe in it with all your heart, then go out and start making your intention a reality by working at it!

The same goes for anything you'd like to manifest. How about...happiness? If that sounds good, it's probably because you're not happy now. How come? What's missing in your life that's keeping you from being happy? And please don't tell me it's money.

You *can* manifest changes in your life, minor ones that will make all the difference.

Are you trapped in a bad relationship? What's wrong with it? Can it be fixed? Is it worth fixing? Do you care enough to want to fix it? If not, then get out. Get the elephant off your foot!

Hate your job? Get a new one. I can hear you moaning already. Hey! Who said it was going to be easy? Easy is empty! Easy is devoid of personal satisfaction! Of growth! You did nothing to earn it!

Living is a full time occupation! It takes work!

Begin with intending small manifestations. Begin with things you have some control over. You are from the Sun! Begin!

You now know how to bring its unlimited power into your being! Use it as your generator. Use it to fuel your intentions through the exercise of your will and imagination, and from there into your acts of manifestation! Do it!

Chapter 8

MEN'S TRUE POWER

Intention

I intend sanity and stability

The female ultimately has the power on this planet. The male is the Love source, not the Power source. If you look at most women, and see how angry they are, it's because they've been put in a position of having to be lovers instead of the power brokers, which is what they are. And men have had to become power brokers instead of the lovers that they naturally are. It's upside down. Males should be wearing pink, females should be wearing blue, because that is the vibration for a woman. And the vibration for man is pink.

This will be a difficult concept for men to accept, that having power is not in their true nature. Yes, being the Warrior, the Guardian is a phenomenal power, yet with a different intention.

With men, this power, this fire, moves through the heart, and is more electric and celestial. With women, it moves upward through the earth and is grounded with magnetic power. Unfortunately, the true concept of power has become so subverted—by the media, by society—that men have been brainwashed into thinking they have to have power. It's not working. The female, because she's so closely related to Mother Earth, is physically the strongest. Face it! Women live longer. They give birth. To conceive and carry a new life inside them requires enormous strength. Understand what the concept of "strength" really is.

Men are the courageous guardians and protectors here on Earth. It's programmed into our genes to play that role. But somewhere along the way, we got cut off at the knees, an amputation that severed the connection to our feelings. And since we, as men, don't have access to our hearts or feelings because it hurts to go there, we can't free ourselves.

Men Are From the Sun. Women Are From Earth.

Many of us are linear thinkers, so when I say something like, "You are from the Sun," or, "The Sun is your father," you may well respond with, "What? You mean it wasn't Ralph?" Instead, think of the Sun as sending "information" for things to develop or transpire. The planet "knows," due to this information sent from the Sun, how to, for example, perform photosynthesis. While you may not do it consciously, you also process much of this same type of "information" from the Sun. I suggest that you do that *now,* do it *with intention,* the same way you were taught certain knowledge subconsciously by your biological father. It's knowledge you may now have come to realize is valuable information.

The Sun is another father imparting information to all who would process it. When this information, this solar wisdom, is accepted, processed and valued with intention, more information is unlocked and made readily available for use by those willing to accept it.

So visualize very broad, life-giving golden light as being intentionally delivered to you from your father through Son/Sun energy. All yours! And the value of that energy is beyond imagination! There is not enough money in the world to purchase it! It is a true gift, freely given, from the Sun (the Father) directly to you (the Son). It is truly free, life-giving, life-enriching information. This Sun energy is what you are made of. You are at once the Father, and you are the Sun/Son. You are a facet of all that is!

It's called Mother Earth, not Father Earth. Women are attached to this planet in the most basic and profound manner. The earth's energy flows upward through the female body and settles in her solar plexus. Her guts. The center of all feelings and intuitions. It is, by its nature, magnetic.

Men come from the Sun, and for them to get to their hearts, they have to first activate their intuitive guts, which in turn activates their feelings. Going directly to their hearts would be too painful. These steps need to be taken with love and with care.

For most men the path of personal growth has not been a priority. Women, if they can release their anger, can help. Women have access to their emotions, and they know how to reach them. If they will open their source and lead the way, they can help men, providing of course that men are also willing to make the trip. This will be freedom for the male spirit!

By placing the female in the guardian position, her natural role is perverted. She and her children were intended to be guarded by the man, not do the guarding. But in this case, she can become the liberating force by helping men access their emotions, helping them with the pain that step is going to require. It gets complicated. We live in a patriarchal society, and the male love factor, which is so incredible, has been subverted into a need for power. Women are angry because they're not allowed to exercise their power, which is the magnetic intuitive strength of the earth. Men, power is not what makes you happy.

Men Are the Lovers

The truly sad thing is that men cannot ask for love. This is a major problem because it causes such internal conflict in males. Do you know any man who can say, "You know, I really need some love right now." They can't get those words--that need--out there because they've been so brain-washed by this whole power bullshit. Men can't ask for the very thing that they need the most. Women do, all the time; they have no problem asking for expressions of love from the man in their lives. "Why didn't you give me this? Why didn't you give me that?" They bitch about this all the time. "You don't love me enough!"

Women have power and men are the lovers, but they're in conflict because each wants what the other has. Men are told they want power, and women are told they want love, the exact opposite of their natural roles. Mammoth conflict! Everyone wants love!

If you really want a clear, unprejudiced look at the natural roles of males and females, ask a mother who has children. Ask her who's more loving, more affectionate. It's the boys.

Men want control because they are naturally protective. But ask a man who the seat of power is in his home, and the honest ones will say it's the woman. That's it. The "seat" of power. Women "sit" on their power because that's where it is. Men don't. They're the aggressors. The real power of love is the most powerful force on this planet! Nothing else comes even close! Love is the building block of every cell in your body, and of everything else in this universe! What could be more powerful than that?

All you have to do is step back, take your first uncluttered look at what it is that makes the world go 'round, and the truth will become instantly clear to you! A truth that will help you realize your true male role as lover protector, and seed bearer of this earth.

Look, consciousness today is immense! It's not just technological consciousness. It's a huge, galactic consciousness, accelerated beyond anything you can imagine. The sun is accelerating it. The sun is sending out gamma rays as we speak, rays which are stimulating everything and everybody, from a plant, to an ant, to you. We know something is happening; we just don't know what it is. But it's happening across the board everywhere.

Why is everyone so much more sexually turned on these days? Why is Viagra flying off the shelves? Because the sun is turning them on! Everyone's intelligence and intuition is being amped up!

And sure, television and advertising might have something to do with this, but what do you think is more powerful? The sun, or a commercial on TV? STOP BEING ELECTRONICALLY CONTROLLED!

A while ago we were talking about your Magic Wand. The more time you spend watching TV, the less you're going to use your wand. Lose the set in your bedroom. Have a room for the television and reserve the bedroom for its intended use. It is your sacred sanctuary, your cosmic connection, your place for tranquility leading to blissful sleep and…for incredible love making!

You are given one body. One. You think maybe it's a good idea to take as good care of it as you do your car? You get your wheels serviced on a regular basis, right? You make sure it gets the right fuel, right? Wash it. Polish it. Are you making sure your body is properly tuned? Does it get the right fuel? Is it clean? Does it smell nice?

This is a frequency cleanse as well as a physical one. How important is getting some magic in your life? How badly do you want it? Badly enough to work at getting it? We told you early on that this was going to take some real effort on your part, and if you're not willing to take some serious steps in that direction, toss this book right now! We have nothing else to talk about. But if you do care, if you are interested, read on.

Intend, "I am a magical being!" and mean it. Intend, "I have strength and vitality!" and not only mean it, but feel it! You will be able to do this because you're going to be using the most powerful computer on the face of the earth. Your mind! This amazing organ that you neglect every time you sit yourself in front of the TV, play a video game, visit websites, or do anything that places you in a spectator role instead of a participant role. Instead of being a hero in your own self-generated show! Doing anything that numbs down your internal computer in favor of external stimuli.

THIS IS IMPORTANT! THIS IS VITAL! When you begin to exercise your mind, everything else pales in comparison at that point. You become the owner of your mind! The only limit is your imagination, the one we are now working on to get you more flexible, so as to venture into areas where perhaps it has never been before. There is no more exciting journey!

Now it's my turn to ask a question. Can you see your penis when you're standing up, or is your gut in the way? End of question.

Understand: this is about effort, the expansion of physical effort to get your bodies back in shape. It's all one deal. Physical. Mental. Spiritual. For you to begin Intending should be easy. For you to start your Spiritual cleansing is going to also take some effort. Making physical changes will take more effort still, because it hurts. So find what best works for you, and have fun doing this.

Now that you are in the process of creating your new reality, of *Visualizing* this new you, then changing how your body looks will be the most obvious physical difference you can make! "I intend to sculpt my body!"

Men and Women Can Be Equal Partners

As we've said, we're trapped in a Data Society, overloaded with stacks of information we can't process. Too much. Too fast. But men feel they have to try. They have to somehow get a handle on this mess or they'll lose control, and we all know how men feel about losing control.

Men are, by nature, the Love Force, and because of that, men are by nature tender-hearted. If men start using their intuition and start dealing with their frustrations in life, they can then begin easing their way into their hearts. Up until now it has been too painful for men to access their own hearts! So what do they do? They build these horrible iron crusts around themselves for protection. They fear their anger, their loss of control, even their dying, because the pain is too much, too real. "I intend to release fear and anger."

Prisons are filled with men who became enraged when they felt they were losing control. They hit somebody. They burned down a building. They shot somebody. All over the perceived loss of control. Men are, at some level, acutely aware that they are quite capable of doing something horrible if they feel control slipping away from them. So much is tied to keeping it. Knowing that, they are in a constant inner struggle to hold on, stay in control, no matter how small that island of control might be. It's *their* island!

We just talked about being trapped in a Data Society. By its nature, data tends to separate people. As we move into a Perceptual Society, our awareness is being accelerated, and the rules are changing quickly. New awareness, together with huge solar flares, are speeding up time on our planet.

As people in their 70s and 80s die, and the generation behind them moves up one rung on the evolutionary ladder, the Data Society is going to slowly start giving way to a Perceptual Society. We will always have data because it's needed, but not to the exclusion of everything else, such as an increased level of perception.

This next generation HATES the term "Senior Citizen." It hates it with a passion. They won't allow themselves to be called that. They will find a new, sexier term because that's not how they "perceive" themselves. Plastic surgeons are going to make a ton of money, as will any product that makes people look younger.

As we move into this Perceptual Society, we—men and women both—will learn that it's less stressful and more productive to work together as equals, sharing our strengths.

Things got turned around when females stopped putting aside the fact that they are powerful beings. That first demonstration of female independence threw men for a loop that they haven't recovered from yet, and it isn't getting any better. This resurgence of female power has put the male completely off balance. Men must become heart-connected. There are reasons why so few men are in personal growth. As they become more in tune with their emotions, and risk the heart pain that it entails, they will take their rightful place as nurturers, as guardians--protecting with love, releasing their need for incorrect power.

Men will begin feeling more confident, and it takes a confident man to be willing to share control with a woman. Women have become crippled by their anger, victims of subverted power. As women free themselves, they will also help men to rid themselves of negative forces and influences. To realize that rather than being a threat to each other, these men and women will *finally* become true partners.

Men! We are a gigantic power source! Nothing is more powerful than the Sun! Nothing! Without it, we would all die. Every living thing on this planet would die.

By learning to channel the power of the Sun through our bodies, and direct its limitless energy to that part of ourselves we want to make stronger and more intuitive, more sensitive and healthier, we will be exercising a power unlike anything ever experienced before.

By being afraid of losing control, of losing territory, of losing religious beliefs, of losing political systems, look what men have

done to this planet. Look what they have done to the environment. To the water we drink, to the air we breathe.

By slavishly, blindly following ancient traditions based on
fear of losing control and the need to prove dominance, men
have brought planet earth to a point where recovery may not be
possible.

Do you suppose things might be a bit different if men were
operating from the heart, from the Sun, rather than from a lust for
power? For control? "I intend freedom!"

We're asking you, out of love, with positive intentions, to
take control of your life through self-will and the good will in
your heart. Open the lines of communications with your family,
your friends. Have conversations. Men are from the Sun, women
are from the Earth. Can't you see what a perfectly harmonious
balance that is?

What I'm intending, men—including you—what I'm intending is that men will take a moment to step back and alter their
perceptions of themselves. Their current view is so terribly
distorted, and so much less than it can be, should be.

You were asked to find a quiet time, to sit in a comfortable,
straight-backed chair, and relax. Clear your mind of the inner
turmoil and garbage, and begin bringing the Sun into your body.
See the golden stream of energy entering through the top of your
head, feel it moving through you, feel it warming your brain
center. Your heart center, your stomach, your genitals. Feel it
working on that part you want to make stronger, wiser, more productive, sexier. This is the beginning of your journey. By taking
this simple non-threatening step, you have in reality taken a giant
leap forward. You are demonstrating the courage to do something you might have found totally foolish before you began
reading this book.

By making strong, positive intentions, you will be taking
another step along this new path you've decided to walk along.
By believing, with all of your masculine heart, in these steps, you
will begin feeling the results, the subtle changes in your attitude,

in the way you relate to others, and most especially in the way you relate to those closest to you. You will not feel less a man for doing these exercises, but rather more, because by allowing the energy of the Sun to move through you, to become you, you will grow stronger, more confident, more loving—in short, more masculine—and thus begin to activate your higher self. This will wake up your intuitive center and connect you to the earth.

Intimacy

How about intimacy? Feel the fear (hackles) rising on your neck? Believe it or not, intimacy has been as tough for women on this planet as for men. Her dilemma is equally as great.

If the woman won't receive, then she cuts herself off from the strength and fulfillment that a man gives to her. She loses her chance or ability for intimacy. Women have been taught to fill the needs of men—to manipulate them. How happy has this made them?

This condition can only be changed when an element of trust, honesty and vulnerability is established, and the healing energies strengthen their bond and connection. Knowing that one can be vulnerable, that it's okay, that it's a good place to be open, so that energy can occur and heal. Then these two people can start spinning in harmony. They create a divine energy.

"I intend that divine energy flows through this relationship."
"I intend that no abuse energies be woven into this relationship."

Men, how about finding the woman whose mission, clear vision—plus her life style—enthuses you? Her purpose arouses and intoxicates your creative energies and swells you beyond yourself! You want her beingness and qualities in your life. To touch, feel and flow protective energy around her. The confident male has this to do for the female.

Then you, as men, can become the truly awe-inspiring being, with your mind and deeper intelligence and emotional body turned on, with your physical body in excellent condition.

You bring new choices to the planet as a friendly loving guardian.

You bring love back to Mother Earth and to the feminine spirit.

You will wake up the blueprints in your DNA and genetic codes, bringing in information, remembering the accumulated experiences and knowledge from your ancestors.

Your imagination and clear intent, along with your will and desire to create your own reality, will be realized.

What an incredible biological organic computer! And best of all, what a true human being!

"I intend to give myself permission to need love."

"I intend to give myself permission to desire love."

"I intend to give myself permission to allow love."

Chapter 9

DAILY ROUTINES

Intention

I intend to honor myself

Physical Exercises

We've gone through a series of mental exercises designed to focus the Sun's energy on various parts of your body, your mind, your imagination. I'd like to share a couple of physical exercises with you that will do wonders for your body, and as a side benefit, also further sharpen your mind. They can be done anywhere, any time.

Spinning

Exactly what the name implies. You're going to be in a standing position and spin. This exercise will help your circulation, which in turn provides added fuel to your brain. It will tone your arms, aid in the flow of cerebral-spinal fluid—which also helps your brain—and will reduce headaches. By the simple act of spinning, you're creating a vortex which will activate your endocrine system as well.

Starting off your day by spinning will get your juices flowing and focus your mind as you make your intentions. Consider what's happening here. You're beginning your day by doing something you've never done before: standing up and spinning around. The mere fact that you've made the commitment to do that is already a major step in manifesting your new self. Here you are, spinning, breathing deeply, making your intentions, focusing your mind, believing that those intentions will happen, and that as you venture out into the world that day, you'll feel slightly different. A difference becoming more obvious each day.

All of these new techniques you're using will feel strange at first, but with each passing day, they will become a part of your daily ritual. And your sense of yourself, your image of yourself, will change. And you won't be the only one noticing those changes. We did mention charisma before, right? Yeah, we did. Okay, let's start spinning!

Stand with your feet slightly apart so you're well balanced. Begin by clasping your hands together as if praying. This lines you up electromagnetically. Then hold your arms out to your sides and horizontal to the floor, palms facing down. Your shoulders should be relaxed and your arms in line with them. Now begin spinning in a clockwise rotation. Always clockwise.

If you've never done this before, which I'm assuming is the case, pick an object at eye level ahead of you before you begin spinning, keeping your eyes locked on that object as long as you can as you turn, then snap your head around and find it again. Ballet dancers use this technique, which is called spotting, to keep from getting dizzy.

Begin by spinning slowly, and if you do feel yourself getting dizzy, stop and take deep breaths. Don't push yourself. This is meant to be fun, not make you sick. Find a beginning speed that doesn't make you dizzy, then as you get used to spinning, you can gradually increase your speed. But ALWAYS slow down and stop the moment you begin to feel dizzy.

You can begin by doing three clockwise rotations, then gradually build up until you're doing 33 rotations.*

Keep your deep breathing going the whole time. When you finish, jump up once, then again bring your hands together, and make your intention for the day. In the back of this book, I'm going to list several intentions, but you should feel totally free to come up with your own.

A WORD OF CAUTION! Certain health conditions, such as multiple sclerosis, Parkinson's or any Parkinson's-like disease, including Meniere's disease, vertigo, or many heart conditions-- can be aggravated by spinning. So please check with your doctor before you do this exercise.

*From Peter Kelder: *Ancient Secrets of the Fountain of Youth.*

Rocking

Like spinning, this one is easy, and like spinning, it has some great benefits. Find a soft surface; anything with a carpet is fine, just as long as you're not on a hard floor. Lie down on your back, lift your legs and clasp your hands together under the fold of your knees. Bring your chin to your chest and begin rocking back and forth. The full motion should go from having your shoulder blades touch the floor as you rock backwards, to having your tailbone touch on your forward motion.

There will be no dizziness involved with this one, so it should be easy for you to build up to 12 back and forth rocking cycles, which is all this exercise requires.

Benefits will be to your back and to an increased flow of your cerebral spinal fluid.

Time your breathing so that you're inhaling as you rock back, and exhaling as you move forward. Be aware of the pressure on your back; feel it getting stronger. If at any time your back is bothering you, find a quiet spot and rock. "I intend that this pain will go away." The same goes if you are facing a stressful situation. Get off somewhere and rock. It'll only take a few minutes, and when you're finished, you'll feel physically refreshed and mentally stronger. "I intend to deserve."

A Place Just for You

For some of you this might be hard, but I hope you can work it out. Find a tranquil spot in your home, and make it into the space where you practice the things we've talked about.

Ideally it should offer a form of sanctuary. It should represent commitment to your new Life Path, to the creation of your new reality. All you actually need is a corner where you might have some candles, maybe a few stones, perhaps a pretty bird feather, and a carpeted floor to rock on. You can also include photographs of people you care about. This is serious business, and deserves serious consideration. And use some incense. It helps your concentration.

The creation of your new reality is something we've touched on before, and something we're going to touch on again because it's so important.

You currently have a picture of your reality, your belief system, one you pretty much take for granted. You've come to accept it along with the limitations it places on you. Limitations you are quite possibly unaware of. Restrictions placed on your reality by society, customs, friends, acceptable behavior. Think about those for a moment. The things you've always wanted to do but...but were kept from doing for whatever external factors and reasons.

By creating your new reality, you're going to be able to access the freedom and gain the power to explore. To venture into areas you've been curious about, but were either afraid of or didn't know existed.

Your feelings have a great deal to do with your reality. Your feelings--or perhaps better said, your lack of feelings.

From when they are little, there is a terrible separation between male children and their feelings. "Boys don't cry." By implication, that also says boys aren't supposed to express their emotions. That horrible intrusion into their crucial emotional growth period marks them permanently. It's what is behind labeling certain films as "a woman's picture." Men aren't going to like this particular movie because it's about emotions! Men are too tough for such nonsense. They want action! They want things blowing up! They want sex! They want naked female bodies! But emotions? Are you kidding me? That's for sissies!

Isn't it time you stopped cheating yourself? Isn't it time you stopped suppressing the very real emotions you so often feel but do everything to hide? Do you have any idea how attractive it is to a women to be in the company of a man who is man enough to show his emotions? A man who can cry at a sad ending or tender moment in a film?

Releasing your emotions is part of what this book is about. That is just one step along the way to creating your new reality. The liberation of your innermost feelings! The wonderful freedom to feel!

It isn't going to happen overnight, but it might happen as quickly as a flash of lightning! Once you have allowed yourself to not only feel your emotions, but to also freely express them, you will have taken a giant step forward in creating your new reality.

In an earlier chapter we talked about daydreaming, how it's perfectly okay to indulge yourself in such flights of fancy and imaginings. If humans never dared to dream, where would we be today? Our futures are based on present day dreamers and their dreams!

As we near the end of our time together, recognize that there has been a change in your previous thought processes, concepts of reality.

You have been introduced to new concepts, new possibilities.

You have learned not to say, "I hope," but rather, "I intend." The difference between those two is obvious.

You are a member of the Golden Brotherhood, and as such you have learned you can draw the limitless power and energy of the Sun into your being at any time, and anywhere you like.

You have learned to love yourself, as you *are*. To love yourself as you *will* be.

You have learned that everything you intend, everything you do, you will do with integrity.

You have learned that you are connected to a benevolent universe that loves you unconditionally.

You have learned that through your DNA you are a divine code, an utterly unique individual.

As you begin putting into active practice the lessons, thought processes, exercises and intentions you have learned, you will change. Some of those changes will take time; others you can affect right now. Only you can place limits on your growth, and why on earth would you do that?

A Day in your New Life

As you begin waking up, record your dreams. Write them down or speak them into a recorder. After a week or so go back and review them. They may make no sense to you at all, or...or you may begin recognizing subtle clues, insights that might be of tremendous help in resolving current problems.

Dreams are windows into nonlinear realities. There are no time constraints when we dream. We have absolutely no control over what we do dream, and it is this very absence of control that makes dreams potentially very valuable. They are free of our normal built-in censorship program.

You can make your first intention now, while you're still in bed. If you're in there alone, say it out loud. By verbalizing it, you give it added strength. One that should be made every day is, "I intend safety, honor and integrity as I step into the unknown."

You'll find intentions in another section. Use any that you feel would be guides toward achieving your goals for that day, for helping in the creation of the new reality you're building.

Get out of bed and go to that place that's your sanctuary. Get down on the floor and begin your set of 12 rocking motions. Inhale on your way back, exhale on your way forward.

Stand, take some deep breaths, and make another intention. Get yourself balanced, and then begin spinning. Just a few turns at first, always stopping if you begin to get dizzy.

How long has this taken? Five minutes? Seven? A very few minutes that are now a part of your normal getting-up routine. We're talking minutes. A very tiny section of this day, but a vital one. By simply recording your dreams, making your first intention, rocking and spinning, you have begun the empowering process of creating your new reality. Your new self!

Stand naked in front of the mirror, look into your eyes, smile and say, "I love you," and mean it! Look at sections of your body and say, "I love you," and mean it! Look into your eyes again, make your third intention, and mean that!

Get in the shower, feel the water flowing over your body, run a soapy washcloth over yourself and feel dead cells being rubbed away. Feel clean, fresh. This really is a new body you're cleansing. Not the one you washed yesterday, and not the one you'll wash tomorrow. Your new reality is in the process of evolving, being created...by you! Make your fourth intention.

Have a good breakfast, bless your food, and do not limit yourself as to what that breakfast is. If you always have pretty much the same thing, how about a change? How about having dinner for breakfast? How about fueling up properly for the day ahead. Sure beats toast and coffee.

How do you get to work? Drive? Bus? Subway? If you drive, bless your journey. Intend that the cars around you stay in their proper molecular structure and not intrude on yours, and vice-versa.

On the bus or subway, someone is sneezing or coughing near you: "I intend that I am not available for catching a cold today."

And if you do get a cold, yeah, you won't feel so hot, but use the time away from your normal routine as a mini-vacation. Use it as an opportunity to continue the creation of your new reality.

When you get to work—the office, the classroom, whatever—remember that should you feel even the slightest sense of danger, Red Rock! Schools used to be safe places to go, but not any more. By thinking Red Rock, you can not only create a protective field around yourself, but around anything you ask Red Rock to protect.

A word about Red Rock. It is a protective shield you can put around anyone, anything. If you see someone, a total stranger, and you sense that he is troubled, Red Rock him (or her). If you are seeing someone off at the airport, Red Rock his plane. You get the idea.

If you have a test today, and if you remembered to rehearse it, you should get through it in good shape. Same goes if you have a presentation, or any act that requires your individual action. You've rehearsed it, and by doing that, you've removed the fear of the unknown. You've done this thing before, in your dream state, in your mind, and you succeeded at doing it.

If you know you're going to have to get up and speak in front of a group, take a moment to bring in the golden light. Focus it on your throat, and give your vocal chords the energy they need to be strong, to speak clearly, with conviction and with energy!

As you move through your day, make any intentions you feel will help. And yes, the first few times you do this, it will feel strange. But after the first week or so, every new exercise, every new thought, every new intention, will begin feeling perfectly normal. When you come to this point, celebrate! You're beginning to feel comfortable in your new reality! The one *you* are creating!

If feelings of anger and revenge start whirling around in your thoughts, ask that whoever or whatever has caused you to have these feelings be released in peace!

This is exciting stuff! For however many years you have lived, you have just sailed along, letting other people and outside events mold you. The *you* who is reading these words is a product that you had very little to do with. You have accepted what life offered, and up to now, assumed the rest of your life would be a continuation of that. WRONG!

There is not a single part of your life--not your mind, your body, your attitude or your reality--that you cannot change. Not one! Not the way you look; not how you dress. Not how you interact with others. Not how you treat your loved ones, how you treat the special person in your life.

You will become a better man because you are creating exactly the man you want to be! More understanding. More sensitive. More compassionate. More patient. More loving. You will be free to feel and express your emotions. You'll treasure the amazing gift a hug can give. That getting a hug can bring.

There's going to be more laughter in your new reality, simply because you're going to be a happier human being. A happiness that comes from knowing you are from the Sun, a unique member of the Golden Brotherhood. A happiness that comes from knowing you can draw the energy and power of your father the Sun into your body anytime you like. A happiness and sense of security that comes from knowing you have the protection of Red Rock available every waking minute.

YOU ARE A LIMITLESS BEING! Accept that. Believe that.

While you have come to the final pages of this book, you are also poised at the beginning of a journey that will be life-altering for you if...IF you are willing to take the first steps. Willing to take control of your life.

It's up to you!

The Wizard Within

By now you know that you are the "Golden Brotherhood." The Sun is your generator, your communicator and your mystical father. I fully expect you will now begin to create your own reality, and that common sense will play an everyday part in your life.

However, "outrageous ideas" are our adventures, and they spearhead us to feats of wild and uncanny abilities!

This is about creatorship, energy fields, manifestation, and the tools that will help you build your new picture of reality. I know you will do this with integrity.

This work is aimed at opening the hearts of all men who read this material. Understand: you are *always* safe and protected in a benevolent universe.

You are divine codes with your own unique signatures.

The intentions you make from now on will start transmuting fear into "love," worry into "conscious will," and suffering into "freedom!"

You have the ability to be inspired, and to inspire everyone who crosses your path. For this you need the fire of the Sun combined with the feeling of the earth--making your awareness keener, your consciousness uplifted. This gives you the "wizardry" that will be needed to live with honor on this planet.

Bruno Meyer

INTENTIONS

I intend these intentions to be done in a safe and harmless way.

1) I intend a meaningful life.
2) I intend a healthy and vital life.
3) I intend prosperity.
4) I intend abundance.
5) I intend clarity.
6) I intend success and honor.
7) I intend that I am safe, always. (Red Rock)
8) I intend to create my own reality.
9) I intend to be employed by spirit.
10) I intend Flexibility.
11) I intend to work with the higher dimensions.
12) I intend to open to change and opportunity.
13) I intend to be more compassionate.
14) I intend to be more intelligent.
15) I intend to go beyond ego and logic.
16) I intend to expand my conscious mind.
17) I intend to release worry from my vibration.
18) I intend a loving partner.
19) I intend peace and harmony.
20) I intend to be comfortable with wealth.
21) I intend to thrive.
22) I intend to release guilt.
23) I intend wisdom and insight.
24) I intend awareness.
25) I intend to live with passion.
26) I intend sovereignty.
27) I intend courage and stability.
28) I intend to open my heart through feeling.
29) I intend to bring harm to no one.
30) I intend a joyful life.

31) I intend love and creativity.
32) I intend to release suffering.
33) I intend fun!
34) I intend _____
35) I intend _____
36) I intend _____
37) I intend _____
38) I intend _____
39) I intend _____
40) I intend _____
41) I intend _____
42) I intend _____
43) I intend _____
44) I intend _____

APHRODISIACS

Are there such things as true aphrodisiacs? The answer to that question lies, as do so many others, in the power of the mind. There are people who believe that if they chew on a leaf from a coconut palm during a full moon when it's pouring rain, what they wish for will come true. They believe this with all their heart and soul...and mind.

Traditionally, it has always been the male who searched for something, anything to stimulate his sexual potency. It was he, after all, who had to produce an erection.

We're going to give you some very simple brews you can make at home. The mere act of their preparation should take on the air of performing a ritual. Have some candles around. Prepare the mix with the one you love. Buy a special set of cups and saucers to be used for this purpose and none other. If you smoke, leave the cigarettes aside. Some music would be nice. Soft, serene melodies. Light some incense. Make this a production!

Ginseng Tea

Ginseng root: 1 tablespoon
Ginger root: 1 tablespoon
Licorice: 1 tablespoon
Dates: As desired

Place all of the ingredients in 2 cups of water, bring to a boil and allow to steep. Filter and sweeten with honey.

Damiana Tea

Damiana herbage: 3 parts
Peppermint herbage: 2 parts
Bitter Orange blossoms: 1 part

Mix the herbs and brew in boiling water. Use about 1 heaping tablespoon of the herbal blend for each cup of water. Let steep for 5 minutes. Sweeten to taste with honey or brown sugar.

Cardamom Coffee

Coffee beans: 1 heaping tablespoon
Cardamom: 1 heaping tablespoon
Milk: To taste

Mix the freshly ground coffee and ground cardamom and brew as you would regular coffee. Add the milk, which improves the solubility of the essential oil of the cardamom. Sweeten with honey or brown sugar.

You should always use the ritual we suggested for the Ginseng Tea.

Vanilla

And all this time you just thought it tasted great when made into ice cream. As it turns out, Vanilla can also have a mildly stimulating effect on the motor nerves when used in larger quantities, BUT! Too much can be toxic, so...NEVER USE MORE THAN TWO WHOLE VANILLA BEANS at any one time in a recipe!

Here's a vanilla-based milk shake you can whip up whenever the mood strikes you:

1 cup of milk
15 whole cloves
15 cardamom pods
2 cinnamon sticks
1 vanilla pod, split
1 cup of frozen vanilla yogurt
Honey: To taste

Place the milk, cloves, cardamom and cinnamon into a saucepan; scrape in the vanilla seeds from the pod. Heat the mixture, but do not bring to a boil. Remove from heat and allow to cool, then refrigerate until chilled. Strain the mixture into a blender goblet and discard spices. Add in the frozen yogurt and up to one tablespoon of the honey to taste. Blend until smooth and frothy. Good stuff.

Sarsaparilla

Another hidden little treasure that has been used for centuries in South and Central America, medicinally as a general tonic and a remedy for impotence, as well as a cure for sexual diseases.

The plant it comes from has been found to contain *phytosterols,* the raw material of testosterone and progesterone, along with a cortisone-like *phytohormone* that helps fight infections. There are those who believe these chemicals can be used as safe replacements for anabolic steroids to aid in building muscles.

As a sexual booster, try taking one heaping tablespoon of powdered sarsaparilla, or 10 to 30 drops of sarsaparilla, three times a day.

Licorice

Surprised to find Licorice in this section? As it turns out, the sweet root of the Licorice plant has been used for centuries around the world for medicinal and aphrodisiacal purposes.

Licorice contains traces of *phytoestrogen sterols* quite similar to those produced in the adrenal glands, and when that was discovered, it led to such a craze in Germany that at one time, Licorice overtook chocolate as the preferred lover's gift when women began reporting that Licorice flavored candy turned them on!

The following recipes are an easy and enjoyable way to try Licorice as an aphrodisiac.

CAUTION! Use them carefully, as too much Licorice can raise blood pressure, and may affect the body's potassium levels.

You're going to need both a mortar and a pestle; a food processor won't work.

> 1 ounce of licorice root
> 1 ounce of sesame seeds
> 1 ounce of fennel seeds
> 1 pint of water

Grind the licorice root and seeds together, using the pestle. Bring the water to a boil, add the licorice root and seeds. Boil for five minutes, reduce heat, cover and let simmer gently for 20 minutes. Cool and strain.

Here's another with fewer ingredients:

> ½ pound of dried licorice root, chopped
> 3 pints of distilled water

Put the root into the water and bring to a boil. Continue to boil rapidly until the water is reduced to about 1 quart, then strain. Fill a cup about half full with the mixture, which will be thick and gummy. Fill the rest of the cup with warm water or milk, then add honey to taste.

FREQUENCY CLEANSE

A Cleansing Bath

This is one you can do for yourself. Buy one pound each of sea salt and baking soda from a health food store. When you get them home, keep them separate from each other before using them.

When you're ready, pour both into a tub filled with warm, *not* hot, water. Treat yourself kindly. This is for you. Allow yourself the luxury of at least 30 minutes in there. To let the solution work all over you, dip your head under the water a few times. And sure, it's okay to laugh out loud as you're doing this. Laughter is a good thing. This combination neutralizes harmful X-rays, Etc.

Cleansing and Recharging Techniques for Your Stones

Indians have used sacred herbs for cleansing and purification for centuries. Cedar and sage are the most powerful of the aromatic healing herbs. They can also be used to cleanse crystals. The herbs are set afire, and the sweet smelling smoke allowed to move over the surfaces of the crystals and stones, thus purifying them.

Before and after every crystal or stone healing, use smudge sticks to cleanse the crystals and clear the air.

The wonderful aroma produced by the smoke can be used before you meditate, or in saunas, to purify the environment after arguments or conflicts. You can also use it before you move into a new space to clear away any negative energies that might remain from previous inhabitants.

HERBS

(And a Mineral Cocktail)

Please check with your doctor before using any of these.

Algae

Yeah, that stuff that grows around watery places. Did you know algae is responsible for 90% of the oxygen we breathe? The Japanese, who happen to live surrounded by water, have been eating seaweed and sea plants for generations. They enjoy the highest longevity rate of any culture. We're at #11.

Sea vegetables are great at purifying, cleansing, nourishing and rebuilding your entire body system. They alkalize the body and transform the many toxins floating around in there into harmless salts, which the body can then easily dispose of.

It also has the unique ability to bind heavy metals and radioactive substances to their own molecules. This is important because the alginate cannot be broken down by saliva or bile, and thus cannot be absorbed into the body, and is instead secreted from the body, together with the heavy metals and radioactive substances.

Marine flora possess numerous antioxidant, antimicrobial and antibiotic properties, and many contain antitumor agents as well. They offer protection from cancers of the digestive tract by swelling the intestines and diluting potential carcinogens.

Research supports the conclusion that because seaweed contains the active ingredient *fucoidan*, it is associated with a reduced risk of breast cancer.

Other studies have shown that another constituent, the *sulfolipids*, protect human T cells from being infected by the AIDS virus.

I know you've heard how important the antioxidant *beta-carotene* is in reducing free radicals in your system. But did you know it's abundant in blue-green algae? Now you do.

Algae is close to being a perfect food. It has a wide variety of vitamins, minerals and amino acids in a balanced and highly assimilatible form. Most dried seaweeds can be stored for years and not lose their potency. Perhaps if you add some to your diet, they'll help keep you from losing yours.

Bilberry

This is another antioxidant that helps inhibit free radical damage in human tissue.

In Europe, *Bilberry* is the most frequently prescribed medication for the treatment of eye disorders and the maintenance of healthy vision. It helps the eyes adjust more easily between light and darkness. Great for driving at night.

The studies on its use as an anti-ulcer agent are very promising.

Cat's Claw

A strange name, which is translated from the Spanish, *uña de gato*. This herb is causing quite a stir throughout the research community.

The *polyphenols* in Cat's Claw make it a very powerful antioxidant and immunostimulant. Along with its many exciting characteristics, it also helps the body deal with stress, a factor we are actively looking to reduce in your daily existence.

As if all that weren't enough, researchers are investigating Cat's Claw use as a possible cure for certain kinds of cancer and AIDS.

It is also an anti-inflammatory, and acts as a natural steroid.

Cayenne

The remarkable healing properties of Cayenne are so numerous that it is routinely included in any top ten list of herbs.

It is thought to improve circulation, fight fatigue, help rejuvenate and cleanse the entire body, stimulate blood flow to the brain, aid in digestion, and equalize and strengthen the heart and nerves.

Administered in low doses, and checked to see what dosage is right for you, along with proper nutrition, Cayenne has produced hundreds of ulcer cures.

Echinacea

You have probably heard of this one. It's one of the most powerful immunostimulants around. If you feel a cold coming on, this is the one you take first.

It's also well known for its actions as an antiviral, antifungal, and natural antibiotic. Echinacea is also considered to be a blood purifier. It speeds up the blood flow through your liver, thus helping to clear out toxins. You really should have this one in your home.

Garlic

Folks in Mediterranean countries really love garlic, using it in everything they cook. Interestingly, people from that region have such a low rate of heart disease that researchers are now studying its role in the circulatory system.

One of its principal constituents is the *thiols;* these block the enzymes that promote the growth of tumors, particularly in the colon, lungs, stomach and esophagus.

A study by the National Cancer Institute showed that people who include garlic and onions in their daily diet lowered their risk of stomach cancer by 40%. I love this! Something that makes foods taste better is also good for you!

The two antioxidant minerals in garlic, *selenium* and *organic germanium,* are easily assimilated into the body. It has quickly become America's number one alternative for lowering cholesterol and reducing blood pressure.

Garlic protects the liver from damage caused by chemical pollutants and synthetic drugs, and is also a great antioxidant for all cellular membranes. And it is powerful in that it kills off such microbes as vira and bacteria.

Ginkgo Biloba

Another one you've probably heard of. It's considered brain food because it does provide nourishment to that organ, and because it has demonstrated that it offers relief from memory loss and the ability to concentrate.

What has become quite clear is that Ginkgo increases the quantity of capillary circulation, thus also increasing blood flow to the brain, the heart, and other organs.

One study found that Ginkgo prevented radical damage to the kidney and liver normally caused by the use of immuno-suppressive drugs following transplants. This finding may make it useful in the future to prevent the body's normal rejection of transplanted organs.

Ginkgo Biloba has been used by much of the world's population for hundreds of years. So even if it does not prove to be the wonder drug that will one day help cure Alzheimer's, it will still remain a valuable herb for its antioxidant properties.

Ginseng

Traditionally, Ginseng has been used to invigorate the body and calm the spirit. It also improves both mental and physical performance, and is helpful in the recovery from any kind of debility.

In Eastern lands Ginseng is prized for promoting longevity and increasing resistance to disease.

Ginseng is also commonly found in many herbal formulas designed to support the adrenals, because it allows them to function optimally under stressful conditions.

Adaptogens, which Ginseng is, are gifts from the Creator that help us modify the effects of environmental stresses like chemical pollutants, radiation and lousy eating habits. They also help with emotional and other internal stresses that, sadly, are so much a part of our daily lives.

Milk Thistle

Often referred to as "the liver herb" because Milk Thistle helps that organ perform a wide variety of absolutely essential functions. Listing these functions would take several pages, so let's just hit the highlights:

The liver is vital for maintaining healthy blood, gallbladder, digestion and endocrine functions. It is the tireless soldier working 24 hours a day to rid our bodies of pollutants.

A properly functioning liver is really important for people with chemical sensitivities, or for those continually exposed to toxins where they work. It is also a big help in warding off the damage done by the excessive use of alcohol, and the use of antidepressant or anticonvulsive drugs.

Saint John's Wort

There has been a lot of talk recently about Saint John's Wort. At one point, most of the attention was focused on it as a Prozac and Zoloft substitute, both of which are over-prescribed, over-priced, and have long-term, cumulative side effects. But further studies have revealed it has many other healing capabilities as well. In Germany, Saint John's Wort is the most popular anti-depressant, outselling Prozac by seven to one.

Its anti-inflammatory properties make it an effective aid for muscle spasms, back pain, arthritis and sciatica pain.

ATTENTION! Proper labeling is crucial! It should *always* accompany Saint John's Wort and its formulas, especially if taken in high doses. It should never be taken with pickled foods, wine, weight-loss products, decongestants or other antidepressants or stimulants like ma-huang. Light-skinned people may be at risk for blistering, and should not sunbathe when using this herb.

Saw Palmetto

The red-brown berries of saw palmetto were eaten by Native American men to increase sexual vigor. It is a fan-shaped herb that looks like a palm. Saw palmetto reduces inflammation in the prostate tissues and helps reduce cholesterol deposits. Its dieuretic action is one of the best herbs for the prostate.

The Minerals

Here's a mineral-rich herbal cocktail that will do wonders for you. It's great as a supplement for good antioxidant activity:

Combine equal parts of red clover, raspberry, dandelion, rose hips, parsley, yellow dock and alfalfa in a glass jar, then pour boiling, distilled water over it. Seal the jar and shake well over a twenty-minute period. Strain it. You can drink this either hot or cold.

AROMATHERAPY

It's in the name. Aroma + Therapy. The use of fragrances for therapeutic purposes.

If you think about this for a moment, remembering certain odors, you will be transported. Where do you go when you remember the smell of roasting peanuts? Fried chicken? Hot dogs? Wherever you do go, it's a great trip back.

Many essences are natural remedies for helping us manage stress, an old enemy of love. Others have long histories as aphrodisiacs. And we guess you know how crucial scents are as sexual receptors in the animal kingdom.

Scents can create an atmosphere of intimacy between lovers. A good thing.

Used correctly, essential oils can help promote balance between the sympathetic and parasympathetic nervous systems. They also are great boosters of the imagination; they help in restoring peace to our minds, and create heightened self-awareness.

Here is a short list of some of the essential oils that you should have at home:

Jasmine

This one is considered the king of the essential oils that have aphrodisiacal effects. Its warm, heady fragrance is a stimulant, and symbolizes passion and joy. It is thought to help with problems of depression, anxiety, frigidity and impotence.

Sandalwood

The oil distilled from this wood inspires tranquility, and is regarded as a sexual restorative for both sexes.

Cedarwood

This one promotes relaxation, and is included in many aphrodisiac formulas.

Ginger

The Chinese have been using Ginger as an aphrodisiac for over 3000 years. As a tonic, it is recommended to sharpen the mind and soothe the emotions.

Cardamom

It's a member of the Ginger family and has a really nice, fresh scent. Cardamom oil is known as the Fire of Venus, and is considered *magnetic* to the opposite sex.

We have listed these oils here because beyond the aphrodisiac qualities, they can also help with a series of complaints that cause a slow-down in your libido. A bad thing.

Working up an interest in sex is rough when you're not getting enough sleep. And if you're all wound up with anxiety, forget it.

Add about 6 drops of the essence you're going to use to 1/8 cup of a base vegetable oil such as jojoba, soy or grapeseed. This will dilute the oil to a level where you can apply it directly to your skin.

Using Essential Oils

These oils are very potent and should not be applied to your skin without first diluting them. Here's how to use them properly:

You can also add a few drops to things like body creams and lotions, as well as to massage oils. Massaging various essential oils on various chakra points can help free up sexual energy. If you don't know what chakra points are, you should. Get a book; find out.

We've talked about how Frequency Cleanse baths can be a very good thing. Adding a few drops of these oils to your bath water will further enhance the experience.

What you should be seeing by now is that there are many really simple things you can do that will make your life better, both mentally and spiritually. There is only one requirement: you have to use them!

Here's a list of problems you might be having from time to time, and the fragrances that will help you get past them.

Insomnia: neroli, clary, sage, sandalwood, basil, chamomile, lavender, orange, apple.

Nightmares: fennel mint, rosemary, marjoram, orange, mary, heliotrope, patchouli.

Depression: angelica, lemon, ginger, eucalyptus, neroli, parsley, patchouli.

Lethargy: rosemary, ylang-ylang, eucalyptus, lemon, pine.

Stress: rose, tarragon, vervain.

Inability to concentrate: carnation, bergamot, coriander, jasmine, lemon.

Stale or toxic air: basil, peppermint, pine.

A PUNCH LIKE NO OTHER

The next time you give a party, try mixing up a punch using these ingredients. Don't be surprised if the next day you get calls asking what the hell you put in that thing. Tip: You'll get more juice from your oranges if you dip them for a bit in hot water before squeezing them. This recipe serves about 20.

> 2 bottles white rum
> 2/3 liter of a dry white wine
> 1 cup of Triple Sec
> Juice of 10 oranges
> Juice of 6 lemons
> 20-ounce can of drained pineapple chunks
> 1 cup sugar
> 2 split vanilla beans
> 2 ground nutmegs
> 2 ounces of muira puma tincture, preferably
>   in a base of vegetable glycerin and alcohol
> 1 to 2 ounces of damiana tincture
> 2 whole oranges studded with cloves
> A handful of fresh or dried rose petals

Yeah, yeah, it sounds complicated. But trust us, this is a punch that packs a punch!

Put the alcohol, juices, pineapple, sugar, vanilla, nutmeg, muira puma and damiana into a large punch bowl, stir well until the sugar is fully dissolved. Now carefully float the clove-studded oranges on the punch, then just before you serve it, sprinkle on the rose petals.

It's going to look, smell and taste like nothing you've ever experienced before. The women at your party are going to be blown away, and see you through very different eyes. Who's this guy who came up with this amazing looking punch? Wow! Then when they take their first sip, watch the expressions on their faces.

The guys might wonder about those rose petals floating on top, but when they take their first taste, all will be forgiven.

Quick Order Form

Telephone orders: (206) 501-7250

Postal orders: Straz Publications
6920 Roosevelt Way NE, Box 279
Seattle, WA 98115 USA

Name: _____

Address: _____

City _____ State _____ Zip _____

Telephone: _____

Email address _____

Sales Tax: WA residents please add 8% of book price.
Shipping: Add $2.00 to the $12.00 book cost—plus tax where applicable. If ordering in volume, shipping is less per book.

Send check or Money Order.